The Zen of Resume Writing for Formerly Incarcerated Persons

The Zen of Resume Writing for Formerly Incarcerated Persons

Simone R. Richardson

安

Peaceful
Japanese Kanji

iUniverse, Inc.
New York Lincoln Shanghai

The Zen of Resume Writing for Formerly Incarcerated Persons

iUniverse books may be ordered through booksellers or by contacting:

iUniverse
2021 Pine Lake Road, Suite 100
Lincoln, NE 68512
www.iuniverse.com
1-800-Authors (1-800-288-4677)

Illustrations by Simone Richardson

ISBN: 978-0-595-42312-5 (pbk)

ISBN: 978-0-595-86651-9 (ebk)

Printed in the United States of America

Dedicated to the one who found compassion.

Compassion is the foundation of Zen.

Clifford M. Rucker Jr. (Chip)
1949–1998

Be compassionate.

Be a messenger that delivers compassion to everyone—
not through some esoteric practice, but through the
kindness of your eyes.

From The Zen Book, by Daniel Levin

We are what we think.
All that we are arises with our thoughts.
Your worst enemy cannot harm you,
As much as your own thoughts unguarded.
But once mastered,
No one can help you as much,
Not even your father or mother.

Dhammapada, translated by Thomas Byrom, copyright 1993, used with arrangement by Shambhala Publications, Boston, Massachusetts.

Contents

Preface

In 2007 I accomplished 22 years of library work experience. Six years before, as a librarian, I started to notice an interesting trend—a small segment of the library populace began coming up to me requesting job search and job placement assistance. The request is not at all unusual except that the segment of the population I'm referring to are formerly incarcerated persons.

Formerly incarcerated persons are unique because they face many barriers to employment. The barriers to their employment consist of a lack of work experience, poor education, drug and alcohol addiction, stigma and bias.

Many formerly incarcerated persons' records are not a result of violent crimes, but a result of property crimes and drug related convictions.

According to the U.S. Department of Justice Bureau of Justice Statistics over 2 million individuals were incarcerated in State or Federal prisons or local jails in 2005. Many of those inmates were released to the community after serving their time. The estimated time a formerly incarcerated person will re-offend and return to prison is three years. A stable work environment, it has been found, greatly reduces the likelihood of former inmates returning to prison.

After developing and teaching resume writing workshops for the general public, and creating an ex-offender job search resource for the public, and a little coworker encouragement, I found that there was a need for a resume resource for the formerly incarcerated individual. In addition, I also discovered a characteristic that would appear over and over again among some of the participants in the resume workshops—some people were literally stressed over the resume writing procedure. I thus combined my love of Zen, to help people overcome the stress of resume writing; included techniques inspired by my resume writing workshops, and focused the two interests toward ex-offenders to form *The Zen of Resume Writing for Formerly Incarcerated Persons*. I hope you will find this resource useful.

Acknowledgements

I want to thank my mother who always told me to reach for the stars and my late father who taught me to be strong. In addition, I'd like to thank the library General Manager who told me to write a book, and the Technical Services employee who told me to continue my ministry to ex-offenders. Thanks to Del Monte and the library Graphic Artist for allowing me to change and recreate their resumes.

Special thanks to the Electronic Services Trainer for his encouragement and proofreading efforts.

Introduction

The moment you leave those prison bars you must prepare yourself for the job search. The longer you wait to find a job the less productive you'll seem to potential employers. Some employers will consider hiring formerly incarcerated persons if those persons can prove they have taken the necessary steps to rehabilitate themselves and have acquired the skills required for the job. Prison is punishment. It is up to you, the formerly incarcerated individual, to take that punishment and transform it into a rehabilitated person anew—a productive member of society. There are techniques to help you in your job search. One technique is a skillfully written resume. Remember, looking for a job is a job, and because of your status it is not going to be easy, but it will happen. Perseverance is the key—never, ever, give up!

The Zen of Resume Writing for Formerly Incarcerated Persons will not only focus on the meditation process to help you calm and prepare yourself for resume writing, but it will discuss helpful resume writing techniques, basic cover letter writing, interviewing skills, and job search tips. The most important concept this book will leave you is the concept of Zen. Zen is the process of tapping into the true nature of your mind. Zen will help you find peace and tranquility. *The Zen of Resume Writing* will help you "awaken" wisdom, compassion, awareness, happiness and enlightenment by providing peaceful meditations.

When you left those prison bars behind, you probably had a myriad of feelings and emotions flowing through your mind that followed you home. Your friends and family may have noticed a change in you. You seemed distant, angry, afraid, and confused—not wanting anyone to look at or even touch you. You are different because you have carried the past home with you—the prison bars are still in you heart. Acknowledge those feelings for what they are and then leave the bars and those feelings behind. Studies have shown that when the body is in a continuous stressed state, too much of the stress hormone called cortisol invades the body and the body is less capable to fight off disease. Our immune systems start to shut down. To counteract this stressed state, you must teach your mind to always be at peace. Zen will give you that peace.

The goal of Zen is to teach us to leave the past in the past, to calm our mind and body, and allow the future to remain in the future. Zen teaches us to live in the moment. Zen teaches us to love ourselves.

How can you sell yourself (your skills) to potential employers or make your work experience stand out from all the rest, or make your resume cause a lasting positive impression in an employer's mind, unless you first unconditionally love yourself.

Beautiful
Japanese Kanji

1

What is Zen?

Zen translated means "meditation" in Japanese. Zen is the practice of connecting to the spirit-mind, also called the "true nature" of the mind, or Buddha-nature. According to Zen, meditation is the key to this connection. Words, however, cannot completely describe the existence of the Buddha-nature. Buddha-nature is the essence of all things. It is an existence that we all possess. It is invisible. It has no shape or form. Buddha-nature is peaceful, perfect, eternal, pure, limitless, unending, and unchanging. It never goes away, cannot be destroyed, and never dies. Buddha-nature was here before you were born, is here within you now at the present moment, and will exist long after you are gone. Waking up the Buddha-nature brings you closer to enlightenment and an end to suffering. Our Buddha-nature is difficult to tap into because it is buried under layers and layers and layers of our attachments, desires, cravings, ignorance, prejudices, hatred, doubts, and fears. Zen meditations help guide people down the pathway to bring out the spirit-mind or Buddha-nature experience. *The Zen of Resume Writing* will help you "awaken" wisdom, happiness, compassion, awareness, and enlightenment by providing peaceful meditations. Zen meditations will point you in the direction to relieve suffering experienced in your present life. Although Zen may lead you down the pathway to end suffering in your life, the complete end of suffering is not achieved by meditation alone. The complete end of suffering is found (according to Buddhist belief) in the understanding, knowledge, and practice of the Four Noble Truths, and the Eightfold Path of Buddhism.

The foundation of Zen originated from a sect of Buddhism that dates back to Siddhartha Gautama (also spelled Siddhattha Gotama) or Buddha's first teachings. Even though Buddha was not a God, but an ordinary intuitive man of great wealth who denounced his status in order to find an end to suffering, Buddhism is often put in the category of one of the world's five prominent religions. Zen Buddhism can be considered a philosophy, religion, a way of thinking, or a way of life. It doesn't matter what you perceive it to be, what you want it to be, or what you call it.

Who was Buddha?

Around the 5th century BCE a boy belonging to the warrior class of India was born. His name was Siddhartha Gautama. Siddhartha's noble birth guaranteed his future as one of wealth and power for the rest of his days. Gautama grew to be an intelligent and athletic young man, and this pleased his father, King Suddhodana, very much. The king wanted Siddhartha to rule the kingdom one day so the father shielded his son from the harsh realities of life. The result of this shielding in the backdrop of the luxurious palace walls was unrealistic and artificial. As Siddhartha grew into manhood he wanted to experience the outside world for himself—the world beyond the luxurious palace walls. Gautama's father agreed to this arrangement. His father, however, tried his best to manipulate the outside world as well, but to no avail.

On the first day outside the palace the prince saw something he'd never seen before. "What is troubling this man?" Siddhartha exclaimed to his trustworthy servant. Apparently, by accident, Siddhartha witnessed an old homeless man with white hair. The man had wrinkles all over his face and body. The man's back was stooped over from old age. The old man appeared among beautiful young healthy people Siddhartha's father had staged for the prince to see. The servant explained that old age is something that happens to everyone eventually and there was nothing anyone could do about it. Siddhartha was taken aback. Siddhartha could not believe his eyes.

On a second trip to the outside world beyond the luxurious palace, Siddhartha saw a very sick man with soars all over his body resting on the side of the road. The man was foaming at the mouth, and had bloodshot eyes. The man was withered and diseased. Once again the servant explained the scene away by telling the prince that the prince was healthy and should not worry. The sick man's plight deeply troubled Siddhartha.

Siddhartha then encountered a funeral procession on his third trip outside the palace. In the center of the procession was a corpse. The participants in the procession cried aloud and sobbed, expressing overwhelming sorrow. The trustworthy servant explained death as something that will happen to all of us one day. The incident had a lasting effect on Siddhartha.

On the fourth day outside the palace Siddhartha encountered a poverty-stricken man with hardly any clothes on his back. The man's only possession was an empty bowl which he used to beg for food. Despite the man's bleak situation the man exemplified overwhelming peace and joy. The servant explained that the man renounced all material possessions to find spiritual truth and a remedy for suffering.

Siddhartha was beside himself. He had been sheltered and pampered and showered with the best of everything, yet shielded from the true devastating realities of life.

At that moment Siddhartha's life was changed forever.

Siddhartha decided to leave it all behind. He would leave the palace, the riches, the future of ruling the kingdom, even a new baby son in search of the end to suffering.

After trying different things to find an end to suffering, including almost starving himself to death as the other spiritual men of his time did, Siddhartha found that the "middle way" was the beginning to his understanding. In other words, he didn't have to go to extremes and nearly kill himself to find the pathway to the end of suffering.

While sitting under a bodhi (fig) tree, transformed by meditation, Siddhartha finally found the answers to his questions. He discovered the universal law of *karma*. According to the law of karma, where there is a cause an effect will soon follow. Your actions can have an affect on your world and the world around you. The universal law of karma dictates that your actions in this life affect the quality of your next life. He realized that nothing is permanent. Everything in life is transient or passing soon. The leaf falls from the tree, the flower blooms and then withers away; the baby is born, lives to childhood, lives to adulthood, reaches old age then dies. Siddhartha also realized that we are all (from the oxygen we breathe, to the trees that provide oxygen, to the sun in the sky, to the soil in the ground, to the plants that are nourished by the soil and take energy from the sun, to the animals that eat the plants, to the humans that eat the animals) interdependent on and part of one another.

Finally, after a long journey of searching, Siddhartha became "awake"—the "Enlightened One" or Buddha. Through meditation Buddha left the world with special truths to live by to end the suffering experienced in this life—a philosophy called Buddhism. *Dharma* is the teachings of Buddhism.

Buddha
Japanese Kanji

2

Zen Buddhism and the Resume

When you write your resume do not worry about the idea that it will be accepted or rejected by an employer. Don't worry about if it is good enough, written well enough, or will stand out enough among the thousands of other resumes. I'm not suggesting composing a poorly written resume in freehand without typing it or without applying the basic principles of resume writing to it. I'm saying stop worrying. The process of worrying means you have already attached yourself to the idea of failure. The attachment to failure will cause you psychological suffering. Everyone will experience psychological (and physical) suffering sometime in life. Suffering is the First Noble Truth of Buddhism:

Life includes suffering.

Why does writing and having a resume make you suffer? You suffer because you want the employer to like you—to like your resume. You want to have the winning resume. You crave to be noticed. You crave to be the best candidate for the job. You crave to GET a job! You desire to have a good paying job with benefits! Your desire is for the employer to consider your resume and call you back for an interview. Your craving is endless. What if the employer doesn't call you back? Constant craving, and continual longing for more and more, will cause you suffering. In other words, you feel depressed, frustrated, and like a failure when you strive for something and find you can't achieve it, or when you had something and you lost it. You feel hurt, angry, and betrayed when you want someone to like or love you, and they have no interest in you. You feel devastated, hopeless, and confused when someone doesn't live up to your high expectations of them, or when you don't live up to high expectations of yourself. Our urge to "want" is relentless and endless. The result of constant craving (wanting) and attachment to wanting is suffering, which is the Second Noble Truth of Buddhism:

Suffering is caused by craving and attachments.

Follow the resume writing advice in this book and study the examples and techniques carefully. Relate and compare the examples to your own work experience. Write a resume. Check your resume for mistakes and then rewrite your resume. Before you are finished you will have rewritten your resume several times. Try to release yourself from the attachment to failure, and release yourself from the desire or craving to be noticed and liked by the employer so that your suffering can be overcome. We only begin to live life completely when we learn to live a moment at a time, a day at a time, and give up useless craving. To give up craving, to give up unnecessary wanting, means to be completely free from suffering. To forsake wanting does not mean to stop accomplishing or reaching goals, it does not mean failure to write a resume or to create a poorly written resume. To abandon wanting means to put one's wants in perspective, or in a controlled order. It means to satisfy one's needs, and relinquish one's unnecessary attachments and desires because a need can be met (acquiring food, water, shelter), but a want never ever ends.

Overcoming suffering is the Third Noble Truth of Buddhism:

Suffering can be overcome.

How can you overcome suffering caused by the resume? Suffering can be overcome by eliminating the craving and attachment connected to the resume. In retrospect, you must remember to release yourself from the attachment to failure if you feel (because of your ex-offender status) the resume is not good enough. Release yourself from attachment to frustration if the resume is not accepted by a certain employer. For instance, if the first employer rejected it, acknowledge your feelings of disappointment. Let feelings of disappointment go, and then send your resume to the next employer. If the next employer rejected it, acknowledge your feelings of sadness. Let sad feelings go, revise your resume, and send the resume to employer number three. Release yourself from the idea of "wanting" the resume to be the best of all the rest. Visualize that the resume "is" the best of all the rest. You will overcome suffering as a result of not knowing how to properly develop the resume by learning resume writing techniques found in this book. You will overcome suffering as a result of the stressful idea of writing the resume by calming your mind and body before you write your resume with meditation exercises found in this book. Zen teaches us to leave all expectations connected to the resume behind. Don't think about the future in front of the resume; just be one with the resume in the present moment. Once you do all this, your suffering caused by the resume can be overcome—but not completely. Suffering in life, according to Buddhism, can only be overcome by giving up craving and attachments and following the Eightfold Path. Following the Eightfold Path is the Fourth Noble Truth of Buddhism:

Suffering can be overcome by following the Eightfold Path.

Each concept in the Eightfold Path falls under the category of knowledge, ethical conduct, and mental control.

Knowledge
Right Understanding
Right Thought

Ethical Conduct
Right Speech
Right Action
Right Livelihood

Mental Control
Right Effort
Right Mindfulness
Right Concentration

Eightfold Path Explained

Right Understanding—Seeing and understanding things in life as they really are. Right Understanding means not applying our ignorance, our attitudes, and our prejudices to life. Right Understanding means seeing life unconditionally. It means realizing that everything in life is transient or passing soon. Knowledge of the Four Noble Truths.

Right Thought—If you come into a situation with the mindset of hatred, evil, and callousness, your reward is hatred, evil, and callousness. If you come into a situation with peace and lovingkindness, your reward is peace and lovingkindness. Arrange your thoughts accordingly.

Right Speech—Refrain from talking about other people. Do not use abusive or disrespectful language. Do not lie. Do not curse.

Right Action—Refrain from doing anything that will cause harm to others. Do not work in a profession that is harmful to others. Do not use alcohol or drugs. Do not take life away from others. Do not steal.

Right Livelihood—Cultivating the discipline to live a good honorable life. Working in a profession that helps other people and the world.

Right Effort—Are you truly putting enough effort into living your life in a peaceful fashion? Are you striving for mindfulness? Are you following the concepts of the Eightfold Path? Are you truly living life?

Right Mindfulness—Living life in the present moment. Being aware or mindful of everything you do. Paying attention to the here and now. Leaving the past in the past and the future in the future. Being aware of one's thoughts, words, and actions.

Right Concentration—Meditation. Quieting the mind. Uncluttering your thoughts. Focusing on one thing. The pathway to achieving Right Mindfulness. Meditation develops a calm and concentrated mind which is better able to acquire wisdom and enlightenment.

Zen Thoughts

Zen meditations will not only calm your mind and body for resume writing but will help you acquire happiness in you daily life.

Buddhist monk practicing sitting meditation.

3

Shhh! I'm Meditating or Zazen

Before you write your resume, calm your mind and body through sitting meditation.

Find a quiet room. Make sure you are alone. Turn off the TV. Pull down the blinds. If you want you can even turn off or dim the lights. The goal is to create an atmosphere of complete tranquility. If you are a beginner at meditation, don't worry about the details of the technique at first. That will come later. You have what Zen practitioners call the *"beginner's mind."* After much practice you will discover your own Zen. Sit in your favorite chair. Sit with your back straight and both feet touching the floor. You can also sit in the cross-legged *lotus* position on the floor. Rest hands palms up on lap with left hand on top of right hand (if your left hand is the dominate hand reverse the hand position). Allow the tips of the thumbs to lightly touch forming an oval. Lower your eyes or if you prefer you may close your eyes. Breathe in naturally without force. Breathe out naturally without force. Clear your mind of all thoughts. Clearing the mind is difficult at first because the mind tends to wander. Be aware of the thoughts that enter your mind and then let them slowly pass out of your mind. Be aware of the air that flows into your nostrils as you breathe in. Be aware of the air that flows out of your nostrils as you breathe out. Be conscious of how your *hara* rises as you breathe in. Be conscious of how your *hara* falls as you breathe out. The *hara* is the spiritual center of the body. The *hara* is two inches below the naval. Meditate this way for five minutes.

Meditation takes practice. If you find that you can't seem to focus and your mind keeps wandering, use words or numbers to focus on breathing. For instance, during the inbreath say *calm*, and during the outbreath say *peace*:

> Breathe in, *"calm,"* breathe out, *"peace."*
> Breathe in, *"calm,"* breathe out, *"peace."*

Breathe in, *"calm,"* breathe out, *"peace."*
Breathe in, *"calm,"* breathe out, *"peace."*

Or use numbers to count the breaths ...

Breathe in, *"one,"* breathe out, *"two."*
Breathe in, *"three,"* breathe out, *"four."*
Breathe in, *"five,"* breathe out, *"six."*
Breathe in, *"seven,"* breathe out, *"eight."*

Count this way up to 10. After you reach 10 begin counting again starting at number one.

Another name for this type of meditation is "mindfulness meditation" which simply means being aware or mindful of the present moment by using the breath.

You have just practiced Zen which is the practice of quieting the mind. Zen sitting meditation is called *zazen.* The zazen hand position is called *cosmic mudra.* Now you are ready to write a resume. Practice this meditation technique before reading each chapter in this book. Increase the meditation technique by one additional minute with each practice.

Cosmic mudra, zazen hand position.

Health Benefits of Meditation

Why practice meditation for the resume? It is good for your health and concentration. If you are healthy and feeling in a happy and calm state of mind, you are better able to write your resume. According the U.S. Department of Health and Human Services National Center for Complementary and Alternative Medicine, practicing meditation may cause beneficial changes in the body such as reducing the activity of the sympathetic nervous system. The sympathetic nervous system causes the "fight-or-flight" response which increases the heart and breathing rate in the body. Muscles become tightened during the fight-or-flight response because narrow blood vessels restrict blood flow. In addition, meditation may stimulate the parasympathetic nervous system. The parasympathetic nervous system controls the "rest and digest" response in the body. The rest and digest response consists of the slowing of the breathing and heart rate in the body which causes blood vessels to dilate thus improving blood flow.

Zen Thoughts: Right Understanding

If you try to understand the technique of resume writing for what it really is without clouding the technique with your ignorance, attitudes, prejudices, and fears you will acquire the Right Understanding of resume writing. Do not write the resume, become one with the resume.

4

Contact Information: How will the Employer Contact You?

One important aspect of resume writing is the contact information. The contact portion of the resume is located at the very top of the page. There is a cornucopia of different ways to write the contact section. The arrangement of the information is not as important as the accuracy of the content. The contact information consists of you name, current address, current home phone number and email address. The contact information may be written in the following styles:

John Doe
123 Main Street
Akron, Ohio 44301
330-223-4567
jdoe@emailaddress.com

John Doe
123 Main Street
Akron, Ohio 44301
330-223-4567
jdoe@emailaddress.com

John Doe

___

123 Main Street Akron, Ohio 44301
330-223-4567
jdoe@emailaddress.com

John Doe
123 Main Street
Akron, Ohio 44301
330-223-4567
jdoe@emailaddress.com

When typing the contact information type your name in 14 point size to make it stand out from the rest of the text. The body of the resume can be typed in either 10 or 12 point size.

The Email Address

Be aware that the email address in a resume reflects your professionalism. Do not use email names like *hotmama* or *cooldaddy*, for your resume. Use the first initial of your first name followed by your last name as in the John Doe example: jdoe@emailaddress.com. If you don't have an email address, get one. An employer may ask you to send your resume via email. Here are some free email providers to choose from:

AOL.com
Gmail.com
Hotmail.com
Myway.com
Safe-mail.net
Yahoo.com

Use your home phone number in your contact information. Cell phone numbers are not recommended. An employer may call your cell phone at an inappropriate time, or your cell phone may start to "break-up" at the very moment the employer calls you in for an interview. Since many people rely on cell phones in this day and age; however, I will leave cell phone use totally up to you. If you do use a cell phone or home phone number purchase an answering service or answering machine and create an answering greeting with a professional message to receive calls when you're not available:

> You have reached 3-3-0, 2-2-3, 4-5-6-7, I'm unable to answer the phone right now, but if you leave you name, number, and a brief message, I will return your call, thank you.

Zen Thoughts: Right Speech

Creating a professional email address and developing an appropriate phone message for prospective employers is an example of Right Speech in the Eightfold Path.

5

Three Types of Resume Styles

When creating a resume you need two types of information: job data, and self achievement data. The job data contains your employment history, job duties, and achievements related to your work. Self achievement data contains your career goal, any special talents or awards, and any related training or education.

Resumes can be written in three specific styles: reverse chronological, functional, and combination.

Reverse Chronological also called Chronological Resume

In the reverse chronological resume you list your recent job first. The job before your recent job is listed second. The job before the second listed job is listed third, and so on. Include your job duties and employment dates. For example, work experience may be written this way:

Chronological Resume

Work Experience

2005-present
EFG Motors Assembly Plant, Warren, Ohio
Assembler

- Assemble engines in large car department.

- Install anti-lock brake systems in sport utility vehicles.

- Process car safety inspection documents.

2000-2005
ABC Paints Incorporated, Akron, Ohio

Painter

• Invented new color scheme for office conference rooms.

• Painted murals for seven downtown office buildings.

• Developed anti-flake paint solution for wooden porch furniture.

1999-2000
LeVar & Sons Motor Company, Akron, Ohio
Automobile Technician

• Designed side panel anti-theft device for light-duty trucks.

• Invented anti-rust device for metal door panels.

• Improved car door cup holders for passenger cars.

As you can see the most current job is listed first in a reverse chronological resume, while the job before the current job is listed second. Notice in the "2005-present" example that the first words, assemble, install and process, are written in the present tense. These words (or action verbs) are written in the present tense because the employee is still performing these specific tasks. In the "2000-2005" example the first words, invented, painted, and developed, were duties that were performed in the past. All duties performed in the present are written in the present tense. All duties performed in the past are written in the past tense.

In a chronological resume you want to use short sentences and action verbs. Action verbs will be discussed in more detail later in the book.

When to use a chronological resume

• If you worked for two or more companies.

• If you are seeking a promotion in your present career.

Functional Resume

In the functional resume you list your skills and abilities under major skill categories. For instance, if you are an excellent communicator, "communication" is a skill area or category in which you can provide examples of your skill. Skill categories may be written in the following ways:

Functional Resume

Skills and Accomplishments

Communication

- Created career workshops for graduating GED students.

- Taught class on public speaking and presentations.

- Developed job and career search programs for current job seekers.

Training

- Taught library students the elements of Dewey Decimal System.

- Created workshop to help adult learners with basic writing skills.

- Tutored students in resume and cover letter writing.

Management

- Organized maintenance crew of 30 workers.

- Supervised 100 landscape employees.

- Designed and maintained daily work schedules for three janitorial companies.

A functional resume highlights "soft skills" or skills that affect how we relate to one another. The following words are examples of soft skills:

creativity	punctuality
customer service	research
computer skills	scheduling
detail oriented	teaching
flexibility	team building
interpersonal communication	time management
leadership	training
listening	tutoring

management   writing

organization

planning

problem-solving

A functional resume lists the companies you worked for without providing job duties in the work experience section. Why? You are emphasizing your skills in a functional resume. By providing your skills you are also providing how those skills were used in the workplace. The work experience section of a functional resume is simply a list of companies you worked for in relation to your categorized skills. Dates of employment are included. For instance:

Functional Resume

Work Experience

Momoko Heavy Equipment Incorporated, Akron, Ohio	2003–present
General Motors Lordstown Assembly Plant, Warren, Ohio	2000–2003
Ling Ling Machines & Equipment, Canton, Ohio	1998–2000

Notice that the work experience section of a functional resume is written in chronological order—the most recent company is listed first. A functional resume is your best selection if you have long gaps in your work history because of your criminal activity or incarceration. Use short sentences and action verbs in a functional resume.

When to use a Functional Resume

• If you maintained long gaps in your job experience history.

• If you lack job experience.

• If the position you want is not related to your current position or experience.

Combination Resume

A combination resume is part functional, and part chronological. The first part of the combination resume is a functional resume. In the first section, list your skills and accomplishments that pertain to the job requirement and arrange those skills under major skill categories. The second part of a combination resume is a chronological resume. List jobs starting with your current job in the work experience section of a combination resume and include job duties. In addition, use short sentences and action verbs. Here is an example of the skills and accomplishments section and work experience section of a combination resume.

Combination Resume

NOTE: The first part of a combination resume is a functional resume

Skills and Accomplishments

Leadership

- Named primary organizer of corporate research programs.

- Expanded survey research team from 10 to 100 employees.

- Selected focus groups for library levy renewal campaign.

Organization

- Designed customer satisfaction surveys for major corporations.

- Created mall surveys to assess consumer buying patterns.

- Prepared statistical reports and submitted to clients.

Research

- Analyzed survey data, influencing fiscal decisions for two companies.

- Provided research data, improving customer satisfaction for major client.

NOTE: The second part of a combination resume is a chronological resume.

Work Experience

2005–2006
Connie May Research Incorporated, Survey Researcher, Akron, Ohio

- Organized survey projects, improving statistical analysis.

- Trained 20 employees on research gathering computer database, increasing research retrieval by 50%.

- Developed new market research procedure for two companies, cutting research gathering time by one hour.

2000–2005
Yolanda & Sushi Research Associates, Survey Representative, Akron, Ohio

- Conducted satisfaction surveys over the phone for five companies, providing information on how consumer products can be improved.

- Created product use surveys, providing data about car baby seats.

- Developed questionnaire rating system from 1 to 10, providing a guide for consumers on best products to purchase.

The combination resume work experience section in the last example exemplifies what employers are looking for in a resume—the "cause" and "effect" relationship. Another name for the cause and effect relationship is the "quantitative description."

The Cause and Effect Relationship or Quantitative Description

The cause and effect relationship or quantitative description of a resume reveals the results of your duties. In other words, what did you do to make the company better? Example:

The Cause
Organized survey projects ...

The Effect
improving statistical analysis.

The Cause
Trained 20 employees on research gathering computer database ...

The Effect
increasing research retrieval by 50%.

The Cause
Developed new market research procedure for two companies ...

The Effect
cutting research gathering time by one hour.

There are instances when employment experience does not always equal results or accomplishments. Do not allow this fact to cause you suffering. If you go to work, complete your required duties, and then go home without feeling you achieved anything don't worry. An employer is mainly looking for how your work experience and skills relate to the job requirements of the company.

When to use a Combination Resume

- If you have many accomplishments to showcase.

- If you worked for many years for the same employer.

Zen Thoughts: Karma and Cause and Effect

The cause and effect relationship in a resume is similar to the concept of *karma* in Zen Buddhism. Karma is cause and effect in Zen Buddhism. In the case of your resume, good deeds at work (cause) result in a better work environment (effect) because you did something to enhance the company.

In Zen Buddhism, karma means action which causes a reaction. Zen Buddhism emphasizes the concept that everything in life is interconnected so if an action occurs in the universe, everything else in the universe feels the effects of that action. According to Zen, karma is neither good nor bad it is just a reaction to an action. This is why you always have to be careful of what you say, think, or do, because your actions can have an affect on your world and the world around you. If you do something positive, for instance, the reaction to your deed may turn out a positive effect on the universe. If you do something negative, the reaction to your deed may turn out a negative effect on the universe. Your actions also affect your *samsara* or present life as a result of endless birth and rebirth. You also have to consider your thoughts in the karma equation. The *Dhammapada* or Buddhist scripture says that "We are what we think …" Everything, therefore, that you have ever thought of has had an impact on your life.

Reflect back for a moment to Right Thought in the Eightfold Path in chapter two of this book. Thoughts represent our actions because a thought may one day manifest itself into reality:

Right Thought—If you come into a situation with the mindset of hatred, evil, and callousness, your reward is hatred, evil, and callousness. If you come into a situation with peace and lovingkindness, your reward is peace and lovingkindness. Arrange your thoughts accordingly.

What Does the Term "Rebirth" Mean?

The foundation of Buddhist belief encompasses the idea of continuous life cycles also called *samsara*, or the endless cycle of birth and rebirth. Another way to interpret samsara is to say our present daily life as a result of the process of birth and rebirth. In other words, when a person dies life begins anew on earth. Suffering also begins anew on earth. The process of birth and rebirth stops when a person gives up constant desire and attachment and reaches total enlightenment (the complete end of suffering) called parinirvana. Zen Buddhists consider rebirth as just another state of existence. In Zen belief, to be reborn is to become one with all things.

Nirvana (the giving up of attachments and desire) can be reached by following the Four Noble Truths and the Eightfold Path.

Work Experience While Incarcerated

Work experience, if it relates to the job requirement of the employer, acquired in prison can be included on a resume. Do not use the words "incarceration" or "prison" on the resume. In addition, do not reveal the details of you conviction on a resume. You can discuss aspects of that in the interview. Note the words "aspects of that." Always accentuate the positive, never the negative on a resume. You can write work experience listing the company that has a contract with the prison as your employer (Enelow, 2006, 31). You can also list agencies which have a partnership with the prison:

2000-2005
Department of Parks and Recreation, Orient, Ohio
Grounds Maintenance

• Renovated blighted lots into playgrounds. Assembled playground equipment, removed litter, distributed wood chips, painted trash cans, and cut grass.

Take note that nothing about the above example reveals your incarceration. Discuss incarceration details at the interview.

Zen Thoughts: Incarcerated

We will never be able to tap into our Buddha-nature if our minds are incarcerated with layers and layers and layers of our attachments, desires, cravings, ignorance, prejudices, hatred, doubts, and fears.

Volunteering or Community Service

Volunteer work is an excellent addition to your work experience. Some jobs in prison are not paid jobs, but volunteer activities performed inside and sometimes outside the prison facility. Volunteer experience enhances the depth and quality of your professional history. Whether you tutored adult learners in reading and writing skills, or trained dogs for special needs individuals, the volunteer experience provides an important work history for the employer to see. Volunteer work performed in prison can be written this way:

Volunteer Experience or Paid Work

Dog Trainer, Johnson Special Dog Training Specialists, Leavittsburg, Ohio
2005-2006

- Trained dogs in basic household chores for special needs persons. Chores included alerting owner about phone calls, retrieving items from wheelchair accessible cabinets, and basic obedience training.

Motivational Speaker, EFG High School, St. Clairsville, Ohio 2003-2007

- Delivered motivational speeches to area high school students encouraging young adults to stay in school and refrain from drugs and alcohol.

2000-2001
Literacy Tutor Program, Caldwell, Ohio
Tutor

- Tutored special learning adults in basic reading and writing skills. Assisted adult students with pre-GED testing in social studies and math.

Notice in the above examples that the organizations and agencies that partnered with the prison are used as the employer.

Zen Thoughts: Right Livelihood

Working at jobs that help others—training dogs for special needs people, encouraging young adults to stay in school, teaching special learning adults how to read and write—is an example of Right Livelihood in the Eightfold Path.

Note: *The fictionalized examples above are based on programs that can be found in the Ohio Department of Rehabilitation and Correction. Resume examples are also fictionalized.*

Action Verbs

Everything you learned in school about writing sentences, forget about it. The grammatical standards for writing sentences are completely overlooked in resume writing. Resume sentences use a technique called the silent "I." In other words, the "I" at the beginning of the sentence is understood but not used. Resume sentences, specifically in the work experience section, are short and begin with action verbs. Why? Verbs carry the action in the sentence. Consider the following sentences:

Wrong
I tutored the students in reading and writing.

Right!
Tutored students in reading and writing, improving GED test scores by 90%.

In the above example you will notice that the correct sentence drops the word "I" at the beginning of the sentence. The above correct sentence also exemplifies the cause and effect relationship. In addition, you want to omit the articles "the" and "a" when writing your resume.

Examples of Action Verbs

accomplished	conducted	gathered	lifted
acquired	coordinated	generated	loaded
assembled	determined	governed	maintained
attracted	developed	grouped	managed
authorized	discovered	harnessed	mastered
awarded	distributed	heightened	negotiated
backed	earned	helped	obtained
brought	edited	implemented	operated
built	enabled	improved	organized
campaigned	enhanced	increased	performed
carried out	established	influenced	planned
caused	fashioned	informed	prepared

classified	followed up	initiated	processed
compiled	formed	invented	remodeled
completed	gained	lead	repaired

Zen Thoughts: No "I."

Drop the "I" in the resume and become one with the resume.

Zen Buddhism. No Self

In Zen Buddhism there is no idea of "I" or "self," just as in resume writing there is no "I" at the beginning of the sentence. The "I" is understood but not used in the resume.

In Zen Buddhism the "I" is also understood but not used. In other words, the "I" or "self" is understood to be any entity—any place, any person, or anything. Money is self. A car is self. The jewelry you wear on you body is self. Greed is self. Envy is self. Hate is self. It is the "grasping at self" that causes suffering. The grasping at self leads to relentless wanting and attachments. When we constantly grasp at something or want (especially when we want and cannot have, or when we had something and lost it), or create attachments to experiences by labeling (I'm a failure because I'm an ex-offender) sorrow soon follows. Zen Buddhism teaches us that the "self" is an illusion because nothing in life remains the same. Everything in life is in constant motion (see the *enso* symbol, next page). Everything in life is transient or passing soon—dying. Zen teaches us to be free from grasping by giving up attachments and desire and by tapping into our "true nature" which is found deep within the corridors of our mind.

When we become in touch with the true nature of the mind we will find happiness because the true nature of the mind is perfect, peaceful, calm, and enlightened. To be in touch with the true nature of the mind means to become "one" with everything you do. Oneness means not attaching labels or expectations to experiences, but accepting experiences for what they are. Oneness is the acknowledgement of all feelings and sensations (whether good or bad) and allowing those feelings and sensations to pass away leaving only an empty space. So if your resume is not accepted by an employer do not attach a label to the moment by thinking, "My skills are not good enough," or "I am not good enough," or "Because of my criminal record I'll never get a job." Acknowledge these feelings and allow them to pass away leaving only an empty space. The empty space represents the present moment. Living in the present moment is called "mindfulness." Mindfulness is achieved, in Zen Buddhism, by concentrating on the breath during meditation.

Mindfulness doesn't necessarily have to be achieved while in sitting meditation. Mindfulness can be achieved anywhere: while doing the dishes, washing the car, ironing clothes, preparing food, cleaning the stove, writing the resume, and walking. Allow your daily life experience to become a meditative mindful experience.

The *enso* (Japanese) Zen symbol represents the idea that everything in life is in constant motion. The enso also represents enlightenment.

Objective: What is it?

An objective identifies the job position you are seeking. The objective is located one space below the contact information. Writers of resume resources debate over whether objectives are necessary in a resume. Some say yes. Some say no. The use of an objective is totally up to you. The following guidelines will help you decide if you need an objective.

When should you use an objective?

• If your work history does not pertain to the job position you are looking for.

• If you are released from incarceration and have little work experience.

• If you are only interested in one job position.

The first guideline, "If your work history does not pertain to the job position you are looking for," refers to the example of working in the plumbing profession for 11 years and wanting to go into a different career field—communications, for instance. Your resume reflects experience not directly related to communications; however, you did take a workshop at the local community college on "How to Become a Skilled Communications Specialist." The workshop will be listed in the education section of your resume to show the employer you have some skills in the communications field. In this case, you'll need an objective because with your extensive plumbing experience the employer will not know what your goals are or what position you are seeking. You will also need to emphasize your past skills that are directly related to communication such as: customer service, interpersonal communication, rapport with customers, public speaking skills, telephone etiquette, writing skills, organization, and detail oriented skills. A functional resume may work well in this situation, including more coursework.

How do you write an objective?

When you write an objective be specific and brief. If you know the title of the position, say it:

Objective Stock Clerk

Career Choice: Telemarketing Representative

Focus: Communications Specialist

Career Selection
Bookkeeper

♦ Product account manager in dental products company

Professional Career Choice: Heavy Equipment Operator

Professional Focus: Bookkeeper

Career Scope: Office Assistant

Career Interest ● School Teacher

Professional Career Interest Machinist

Goal to Achieve
Food Service Manager

Goal to Reach: Beautician

Interest: Construction Worker

Career Decision ♦ Mature Adult Activities Director

If you are considering many jobs, and you are not sure of the position you want, do not use an objective.

Zen Thoughts: Objective of Zen Buddhism

The objective of Zen Buddhism is: there is no objective. An objective implies a "want." A want equates suffering. There is no objective because you are already there. You just need to "awaken" the enlightenment within.

Skills Summary

Instead of an objective you can include a brief skills summary in your resume. The skills summary is located at the top of the resume. The skills summary is one, two or if you have many pertinent skills, three lines "introducing" to the employer the summary of your important skills. The summary represents an attention getting device for your resume. It tells the employer what you can do for the company, not what the company can do for you. It only takes 30 seconds for the employer to scan your resume and either accept your resume or place it in the round file (trash), so why not provide your most important skills at the top of the resume before the employer reads the body of your resume?

How to Write a Skills Summary

The summary may be the following:

1. Centered, aligned left, or indented if in paragraph form.

2. One space below the contact information. If you use a title for your summary the title falls one space below contact information. The summary falls one space below the title.

3. Limit to one, two or three lines.

4. If using one or two lines and aligned left, add a period after the introduction.

5. If using one or two lines and centered, omit a period after the introduction.

6. If three lines are used, indent, write in paragraph form, and include a period after each sentence.

If you have a degree or training in a certain area of expertise use that word first:

Carpenter ...

Use a word that connects your job title or experience to your skills:

1. offering

2. providing

3. with

The first two words of your skills summary should say:

Carpenter offering

If possible, include years of experience:

Carpenter offering five years experience in

Finally, list skills that are related to your position and experience:

Carpenter offering five years experience in cabinet making, designing 1880s style furniture, and antique restoration

Remember the skills summary is located one space below the contact information. In the example below the skills summary is one space below its corresponding title. The skills summary may be called: profile, highlights, career profile, career highlights, key qualifications, professional highlights, and summary. Notice that the skills summary in the following example is titled key qualifications:

John Doe
123 Main Street
Akron, Ohio 44301
330-223-4567
jdoe@emailaddress.com

Key Qualifications

Carpenter offering five years experience in cabinet making, designing 1880s style furniture, and antique restoration

Skills Summary Examples

Career Highlights

Telemarketing representative providing five years experience in data entry, switchboard operation, and over-the-phone research gathering.

Career Profile

Legal assistant offering seven years experience in drafting pleadings, research, motion development, Microsoft Word, Excel, and PowerPoint.

Highlights

Librarian with five years experience in reference management, Web page creation, and computer training.

Skills Summary

Bookkeeper providing seven years experience in payroll management, timecard analysis, and QuickBooks accounting software knowledge

Professional Highlights

Paralegal offering five years experience in motion drafting, Westlaw research retrieval, data entry, and report writing

Profile

Public service assistant providing six years experience in switchboard operations, answering phone inquiries, analyzing and solving customer problem account records on computer.

Summary

Cahier offering five years experience in operating scanner register, money management, and handling product exchanges and returns

Key Qualifications

Factory worker offering eight years experience in tow motor operation, heavy equipment repair, and stock room management

Skills Summary in Paragraph Form

Embalmer providing five years experience preparing deceased for viewing. Worked directly with families preparing funeral arrangements. Created client referral computer database.

Dog trainer offering seven years experience in training dogs for special needs individuals. Received "Outstanding Trainer Award." Developed training manual titled, "Special Needs Dog Training."

Bricklayer providing six years experience in constructing security walls for municipal and government buildings. Built chimneys for low-income housing. Primary trainer for new apprentice students.

Skills Summary

Library clerk offering eight years experience in switchboard operations, and ordering library supplies via computer database. Achieved perfect attendance for eight years. Skilled in Microsoft Word, PowerPoint, and Excel.

Professional Highlights

Mechanical Engineering Technician providing four years experience in testing and designing industrial machinery. Eliminated factory defects and inspected factory machines. Developed auto crash test rating system.

Skills Summary using Bullet Points

You can also write your skills summary using no more than three to five bullet points to highlight your skills. Remember, when writing the skills summary in bullet form, think of the contributions you will be bringing to the job. In addition, put a period after each sentence in the summary. In the following example only three bullets are present under the heading "skills and abilities."

Skills and Abilities

- Five years tow motor operation experience.

- Carpentry skills include furniture and cabinet restoration.

- Experience in woodworking and bricklaying participating in 20 school construction projects.

Skills and Abilities

- Three years experience in maintenance and truck motor repair.

- Designed improved starter switch for antique cars.

- Refurbished body frames of historic cars and trucks.

Skills and Abilities

- Moved and delivered furniture for professional moving service.

- Office cleaning skills specializing in floor cleaning, waxing, and floor restoration.

- Maid experience. Provided cleaning services for hospitals, hotels, and 17 private homes. Awarded "Employee of the Year 2005."

Notice in the "skills and abilities" examples that you have a little more freedom when creating the skills summary using bullets. Also, the summary doesn't necessarily have to start with action verbs. The summary can begin with years of experience, the skill, or details about the skill. The skills summary using bullet points is another attention getting device created to entice the employer's interest before the employer reads the main portion of the resume.

Zen Thoughts: Summary of Our Daily Life Experience

Through daily Zen meditations, we can take the summary of our daily life experience (samsara, our daily life on earth as a result of the endless process of birth and rebirth), and incorporate that experience in the Eightfold Path. Through the Eightfold Path we will find enlightenment as Buddha himself found. Buddha realized that the road to enlightenment and happiness could not be achieved by excess, extremes, attachment, fear, and craving. Take excess, extremes, attachment, fear, and craving out of the process of writing and sending out your resume and you will find happiness as an effect of the resume.

References

You do not have to use the phrase "References Available Upon Request" at the bottom of you resume because it is understood that you will give the employer references at the employer's request. You will also list references on the employment application (see Sample Job Application, Appendix: C). The employer may, for instance, ask for references after the interview. Type references on a page separate from your resume. The references page consists of three names, titles, addresses, and phone numbers of people who know you. Do not include the names of relatives.

Example References Page

John Doe
123 Main Street
Akron, Ohio 44301
330-223-4567
jdoe@emailaddress.com

<u>REFERENCES</u>

Joseph Brown
Professor
Perkins College
333 Maple Street
Akron, Ohio 44304
330-222-3333

Sheila Anderson
Guidance Counselor
Karma State University
PO Box 444
Kent, Ohio 44242
330-111-5555

Tom Greene
Postal Carrier
U.S. Postal Service
PO Box 12333
Akron, Ohio 44309
330-656-5555

Education Section

The education section of the resume is the last section to include.

You do not have to list evidence that you acquired a high school diploma on the resume because this is understood. Provide high school information only if the job requires that you need a high school diploma. There are many ways to write the high school information:

Kenmore High School, Akron, Ohio 2001

East High School, Akron, Ohio
Graduated 2000

2005 Firestone High School Akron, Ohio

Any education related to the job looks good on a resume. If you are taking university courses and expect to receive a degree, but have not received a degree at the time you inquire about a job, you can write your education in the following ways:

The University of Akron, Akron, Ohio
Anticipate receiving Bachelor of Arts in Sociology, June 2009

Ohio State University, BS Biology Columbus, Ohio
Scheduled graduation, May 2008

Goal to achieve B.A. in Sociology, 2007
University of Cincinnati Cincinnati, Ohio

If you have taken college courses related to the job but did not receive a degree, list the course of study plus the name of the school:

Kent State University, Kent, Ohio
Coursework in Economics

Ohio University, Athens Ohio
Classes included Accounting, Bookkeeping, and File Management

Youngstown State University Youngstown, Ohio
(35 credits) Chemistry

Mount Union College, two years focus in Mathematics, Alliance, Ohio

If your highest achievement is a bachelor's degree, do not provide your associate's degree. If the associate's degree is directly related to the position you are seeking, however, include the associate's degree.

What if you have no diploma?

If you do not have a high school diploma, do not include an education section on your resume. You want to promote and highlight your skills and experience. Emphasize the positive never the negative on your resume.

Zen Thoughts: Craving

It is human nature to want—to crave. How can we stop "wanting" our resume to be the best? The only way to achieve happiness in this life is to give up constant craving and attachments. To forsake wanting does not mean to give up reaching for goals. To abandon wanting means to put your wants in perspective, or controlled order. It means to satisfy your needs, and relinquish your relentless attachments and desires because a need can be met (acquiring food, water, shelter), but a want never ever ends.

Other Elements Found in a Resume

There are other elements found in a resume. As long as these elements are related to the position you are applying for you can include one or more of them. For example, if you are applying for a customer service position and have taken an educational workshop on the topic, you can list the workshop this way:

Additional Training

Johnson Customer Service Training, 2000

• Completed three day workshop on customer service skills.

In the education section or a separate section, you can also include any license or certifications you may have acquired:

License

HVAC License, State of Ohio, 2004

Certification

Applicator Certification, State of Ohio, 2001

Provide any important professional memberships, awards and military service:

Awards

Employee of the month, 2001
Perfect attendance, 2005

Military Service

U.S. Marine Reserve, 2002-2005

Professional Affiliations

American Welders' Association

American Boarding Kennels Association

Resume Writing Checklist

- **Do not include references on a resume**. Type references on a separate piece of paper. The employer may ask for the references after the interview.

- **Do not include the phrase "References Available Upon Request" at the bottom of the resume**. It is understood that you will provide references at the employer's request.

- **A one page resume is preferable**. If you have many accomplishments to highlight include a second page. On the second page of the resume at the upper right-hand corner include your name and the words "page 2." For example, John Doe page 2, or Doe, John page 2.

- **Exclude wage and salary information on a resume**. The only time you should discuss salary is at an interview. Wait for the employer to bring the topic up. During the interview if the employer asks you about salary you can say salary is negotiable. For salary resources contact you local library (see Appendix: L, Books that Describe Occupations).

- **Exclude personal information.** Your interests, age, height, weight, and marital status do not belong on a resume.

- **Use 8 ½" x 11" quality white paper.** Multi-purpose white copy paper or white laser jet paper is also fine. Do not waste your money on colored paper.

The employer is more interested in your work experience, not the color of the paper.

- **Proofread.** Make sure your resume is flawless. That means absolutely no mistakes. Have a friend read over your resume. Provide plenty of white space (one space separating each section) so that the resume is pleasing to the eye.

- **If you are over 50 do not include dates in the education section.** As long as you have the necessary skills you do not have to include an education section at all. You want to emphasize your skills not your age. Also, do not use dates from the 50s or 60s. Avoid dates from a decade ago and use a functional resume to highlight your achievements.

- **Include years not months when providing dates**. Using the month and the year format (i.e., January 3, 2000) may emphasize gaps in your work history. Try to take the focus of your resume off dates by just providing a range of years worked (2000–2004). If you only worked a couple of months, include just the year (2000). You can explain the details of working for just a few months in the interview.

- **Do not include every job you have ever worked in your life.** You are not writing your life's story on a resume. Only include work experience that relates to the employer's job requirements.

- **Always use typed envelopes to mail your cover letter and resume. Never handwrite the information.** Handwritten envelopes are not professional. Typed mailing labels are recommended.

- **After mailing your cover letter and resume call the employer after a week to set up a meeting.**

- **If the employer doesn't respond after the third phone call spend your time contacting another company.**

  NOTE: For resume examples see chapter eleven.

Recommended Typestyles or Fonts for the Resume

Use typestyles in your resume that are easy to read. Here are a few recommendations:

Ariel, Book Antiqua, Bookman, Century Gothic, Century Schoolbook, Garamond, Gill Sans, Lucida Sans, Tahoma, Times New Roman, and Verdana.

6

Lovingkindness Meditation

An important aspect of Zen Buddhism is its emphasis on compassion for others. One way to acquire compassion is through lovingkindness meditation.

First, focus on the breath by following the sitting meditation technique in chapter three for five minutes. As you calmly inhale and exhale, create a picture in your mind of someone you truly love (a pet, friend, mother, father, sibling, wife, husband, child, or significant other, etc.). Allow the "feeling" of love to remain in your heart as you next focus love or lovingkindness inward toward yourself.

How can you show compassion toward other people if you do not first unconditionally love yourself. The love you have for yourself must also reflect in your resume writing. In retrospect, remember the last paragraph in the introduction of this book:

> How can you sell yourself (your skills) to potential employers or make your work experience stand out from all the rest, or make your resume cause a lasting positive impression in an employer's mind unless you first unconditionally love yourself.

While directing lovingkindness inward toward yourself, silently recite a phrase or say a mantra that stresses your love for yourself. Mantras are phrases or syllables Buddhists use to calm the mind and heal the body. Your silent meditation phrases may go something like this:

> Breathe in, "*I'm happy,*" breathe out, "*I'm healthy.*"
> Breathe in, "*I'm peaceful,*" breathe out, "*I love all living beings.*"

Repeat these phrases for another five minutes while in a meditative state. After five minutes drop the word "I" in each phrase and replace it with the name of a person who is kind or loving to you (i.e., *Fred is happy*). Meditate this way for ten minutes. Traditionally the phrase starts, *May I be (May Fred be)*. I like to use "*I'm*," to represent the present moment.

The last part of the lovingkindness meditation is the most difficult to attempt. Replace the name of the person who is kind to you with the name of someone who is cruel to you. Meditate this way for ten minutes. You can also incorporate in the idea that the person who is nice to you (along with the person who is cruel to you) is free from suffering on this earth. Meditate on this "free from suffering" idea for yourself also. The idea of spreading universal love or lovingkindness (*metta*) is based on Buddha's scripture (*sutta or sutra*) on lovingkindness (*Metta Sutta*).

Over time you will see life in a new happier light. You will discover that old jealousies, grudges, and hatred will dissipate out of your heart, just as the breath dissipates once it has left your nostrils as you breathe out.

Zen Thoughts on Lovingkindness

Zen represents the letting go of unnecessary attachments and desires to make more room for lovingkindness. Expressing lovingkindness toward others brings out our Buddha-nature.

7

E-Resumes

Once you have written your resume some employers may ask you to email the resume. If this is the case, you need to use a text only language application or ASCII (pronounced *ask*). Email operates on a text only language principle. ASCII stands for "American Standard Code for Information Interchange." American Standard Code for Information Interchange permits people with different software programs to understand each other.

Using ASCII is simple. If you are using a word processing program like Microsoft Word, for instance, save your resume as a "Plain Text" document by selecting "File" located at the top left side of the toolbar then select "Save As." You'll see "Plain Text" within the "Save as type" scroll bar.

Once you save your resume in the "Plain Text" format certain characteristics about it will change. Bullet points will turn into asterisks, indents will change and boldface will disappear, what was once centered will align left. It is recommended, therefore, that you write the resume as plain as possible if you decide to email it:

• Don't use fancy fonts.

• Don't center.

• Separate sections with all caps, i.e., WORK EXPERIENCE.

• Place text sections on the left.

• Don't boldface.

• Avoid the use of boxes, lines, and bullets.

To check the look of your resume, email it to yourself. You can also adjust your resume after you saved it in the "Plain Text" format.

Use your other resume—the one with the bullets, underlines, boldface and centered information—when you are mailing the resume, including the resume with an application, or handing the resume to the employer. It is recommended that you also mail your resume if you emailed it to an employer.

Write the resume as plain as possible if you are going to fax it. You should have three resume formats: one ready to be emailed, one ready to be faxed, and one ready to be mailed in an envelope.

Resume before Plain Text

John Doe
123 South Main Street
Akron, Ohio 44301
330-223-4567
jdoe@emailaddress.com

Skills and Accomplishments

Leadership

- Named primary organizer of corporate research programs.

- Expanded survey research team from 10 to 100 employees.

- Selected focus groups for library levy renewal campaign.

Organization

- Designed customer satisfaction surveys for major corporations.

- Created mall surveys to assess consumer buying patterns.

- Prepared statistical reports and submitted to clients.

Research

- Analyzed survey data, influencing fiscal decisions for two companies.

- Provided research data, improving customer satisfaction for major client.

Work Experience

2005–2006
Connie May Research Incorporated, Survey Researcher, Akron, Ohio

- Organized survey projects, improving statistical analysis.

- Trained 20 employees on research gathering computer database, increasing research retrieval by one week.

- Developed new market research procedure for two companies, cutting research gathering time by one hour.

2000–2005
Yolanda & Sushi Research Associates, Survey Representative, Akron, Ohio

- Conducted satisfaction surveys over the phone for five companies providing information on how consumer products can be improved.

Resume after Plain Text

A resume saved in "Plain Text" will end up looking something like this.

John Doe
123 South Main Street
Akron, Ohio 44301
330-223-4567
jdoe@emailaddress.com

Skills and Accomplishments

Leadership

* Named primary organizer of corporate research programs.
* Expanded survey research team from 10 to 100 employees.
* Selected focus groups for library levy renewal campaign.

Organization

* Designed customer satisfaction surveys for major corporations.
* Created mall surveys to assess consumer buying patterns.
* Prepared statistical reports and submitted to clients.

Research

* Analyzed survey data, influencing fiscal decisions for two companies.
* Provided research data, improving customer satisfaction for major client.

Work Experience

2005–2006
Connie May Research Incorporated, Survey Researcher, Akron, Ohio
* Organized survey projects, improving statistical analysis.
* Trained 20 employees on research gathering computer database, increasing research retrieval by one week.
* Developed new market research procedure for two companies, cutting research gathering time by one hour.

2000–2005
Yolanda & Sushi Research Associates, Survey Representative, Akron, Ohio
* Conducted satisfaction surveys over the phone for five companies providing information on how consumer products can be improved.

Now you are ready to copy, paste, and then send the resume through the company's email.

Note: Never send a resume by an email attachment unless the employer says to do so. Companies do not like attachments because they may contain viruses.

8

Keywords

Keywords are the words or phrases that are used in the description of a particular industry or profession. Keywords are useful because some companies scan resumes into special computer software to pick up certain words related to the job requirement. For instance, real estate personnel have to have a working knowledge of local zoning laws, tax laws, mortgages, deeds, a home's market value, and leasing laws. Keywords for the real estate profession include words such as:

Appraisal	Debt
Asset Value	Default
Bill of Sale	Eminent Domain
Blanket Mortgage	Equity
Certificate of Title	Financing
Closing date	Fixed Rate
Holding Company	Property value

To ensure you are using the correct keywords in your resume, analyze and read carefully the description of the job you are seeking. Notice the keywords in the job description. Do you possess the skills of the keywords? If so, include those keywords in your resume.

There are several online and print resources that provide lists of keywords for various professions (see Appendix: K, Keyword Books). Remember, if you describe your job duties thoroughly keywords concerning your past experience will come naturally. Do not use keywords that are not related to your experience just because you saw them in a job description or a book. You may have to explain those words or skills in an interview. Use a keyword resource as a general guide.

Zen Thoughts: Keywords in Zen

The keywords to remember in Zen Buddhism in this resource are: impermanence, karma, Buddha, no self, mindfulness, meditation, lovingkindness, samsara, nirvana, zazen, kinhin, Buddha-nature, enlightenment, Four Noble Truths, and Eightfold Path.

9

Cover Letter Writing Basics

At the top of the cover letter provide your contact information on the right-hand side, centered, or left side.

John Doe
223 South Main Street
Akron, Ohio 44301
(330) 223-4567
jdoe@emailaddress.com

Start your cover letter with an opening statement that explains your years of experience. Your skills summary works well here.

A carpenter with five years experience in cabinet making, designing 1880s style furniture and antique restoration, highlights the skills I'd bring to the Reynard Furniture Restoration Company.

Find out the skills the employer is looking for and use bullet points to emphasize your matching experience.

- Designed special wooden chairs for handicap and wheelchair accessible apartments, resulting in an increase in rental applicants of special needs customers.

- Created and installed cabinets and doors for one story office building, reducing construction time by two days.

- Restored 1880s style furniture for five houses on the National Register of Historic Buildings.

Include one final sentence or two stating you'd like to discuss your contributions further. Include your phone number at the end.

I can contribute a great deal to the Reynard Furniture Restoration Company and would like to discuss in detail how my experience can enhance the organization. I can be reached at (330) 223-4567.

Include the word sincerely or sincerely yours and your name to conclude the cover letter. Sign your name between the words *Sincerely* and your typed name.

Sincerely,

John Doe

Example Cover Letter
Carpenter

John Doe
223 Main Street
Akron, Ohio 44301
(330) 223-4567
jdoe@emailaddress.com

July 3, 2006

Fred Williamson
Human Resource Director
Reynard Furniture Restoration Company
888 Main Drive
Akron, Ohio 44304

Dear Mr. Williamson:

A carpenter with five years experience in cabinet making, designing 1880s style furniture and antique restoration, highlights the skills I'd bring to the Reynard Furniture Restoration Company.

Summary of my professional experience include:

• Designed special wooden chairs for handicap and wheelchair accessible apartments, resulting in an increase in rental applicants of special needs customers.

• Created and installed cabinets and doors for one story office building, reducing construction time by two days.

• Restored 1880s style furniture for five houses on the National Register of Historic Buildings.

I can contribute a great deal to the Reynard Furniture Restoration Company and would like to discuss in detail how my experience can enhance the organization. I can be reached at (330) 223-4567.

Sincerely,

John Doe

Cover Letter Writing Basics

Start of the cover letter by placing your contact information on the right.

Daisy Smith
4566 Barber Avenue
Akron, Ohio 44308
(330) 222-3222
dsmith@emailaddress.com

If you found a job position in the local newspaper mention the name of the paper, the date the ad aired, and the position advertised.

On Sunday, September 9, 2006, in the Akron Beacon Journal, you advertised a position for a Legal Assistant.

Discuss your matching skills for the job requirement.

My five years as a paralegal prepared me for the requirements you are seeking. My experience includes:

- Ability to type 60 wpm

- Westlaw legal research experience

- Report writing

- Investigated the facts of cases

- Motion development

- Data entry

- Computer experience: Microsoft Word, Excel, PowerPoint, Outlook

Conclude by saying you'd like to discuss how your abilities and skills can enhance the company.

Thank you for considering my skills and experience. It would be my pleasure to meet with you to discuss how my abilities can enhance your organization. I can be reached at (330) 222-3222.

Sign your name within the space between your typed name and the word *Sincerely.*

Sincerely,

Daisy Smith

Example Cover Letter
Legal Assistant

Daisy Smith
4566 Barber Ave.
Akron, Ohio 44308
(330) 222-3222
dsmith@emailaddress.com

September 11, 2006

Tom Green
The Legal Team
1111 Blue Street
Akron, Ohio 44308

Dear Mr. Green:

On Sunday, September 9, 2006, in the Akron Beacon Journal, you advertised a position for a Legal Assistant.

My five years as a paralegal prepared me for the requirements you are seeking. My experience includes:

- Ability to type 60 wpm
- Westlaw legal research experience
- Report writing
- Investigated the facts of cases
- Motion development
- Data entry
- Computer knowledge including Microsoft Word, Excel, PowerPoint

Thank you for considering my skills and experience. It would be my pleasure to meet with you to discuss how my contributions can enhance your organization. I can be reached at (330) 222-3222.

Sincerely,

Daisy Smith

Example Cover Letter
Teacher Aide

Betty Brown
124 Palm Avenue
Cleveland, Ohio 44113
(216) 216-2111
bbrown@emailaddress.com

July 6, 2006

Judy Anderson
Adult Learning Coordinator
The Adult Learning Center
3000 East 9th Street, Suite 300
Cleveland, Ohio 44113

Dear Ms Anderson:

In response to you posting of a Teacher Aide, I am offering five years experience as a teacher assistant to enhance your organization.

What you want	My matching experience
Communication	Provided individualized attention to adult students.
Writing skills	Helped prepare lesson plans and instructional material.
Organization	Recorded grades, graded tests, and proofread homework.
Computer skills	Assisted in computer lab. Helped students learn computer software programs.

Please allow me to discuss my accomplishments further. I look forward to discussing how my skills can be an asset to your learning center.

Sincerely,

Betty Brown

Example Cover Letter
Museum Technician

Fred Green
1111 Leora Street
Akron, Ohio 44301
(330) 111-1111
fgreen@emailaddress.com

March 11, 2006

Jane Johnson
Museum Technician Supervisor
Beautiful Art Museum
1112 High Street
Akron, Ohio 44308

Dear Ms. Johnson:

As a museum volunteer for six years I possess extensive knowledge of museum operations.

My career includes experience researching historical information for the museum curator. I also processed and maintained records of the new artifacts for the museum collection. I worked as a tour guide working closely with teacher curriculums to provide an informative and educational tour experience for elementary and middle school students. I restored and installed exhibits for special events and worked with archivists in interpreting and preserving historical documents.

My experience also expanded to the security department where I directed visitors to selected exhibit areas, and protected displays from vandalism.

I look forward to talking to you to discuss how my experience can benefit your organization. I can be reached at (330) 111-1111.

Sincerely,

Fred Green

Cover Letter Writing Checklist

- **Proofread.** Make sure your cover letter is flawless. No misspelled words. No smudges. No wrinkles. No correction fluid.

- **Always address the cover letter to a specific person**. Call the company and ask for the name of the hiring manager, or the human resource director.

- **List any special accomplishment or skills you have related to the position**.

- **A one page cover letter is preferable**. Even if you have many accomplishments to highlight, do not send an employer a two page cover letter.

- **Read the job requirement for the position carefully**. Always match you skills with the job requirements.

- **Always mail or email a resume with a cover letter unless the employer says to do differently. No handwritten envelopes please.**

- **Do not mail in the actual newspaper ad if you find a job in your local newspaper.**

- **Don't forget to date the cover letter.**

10

Zen Walking Meditation or Kinhin

Take a break from your resume writing experience and discover Zen walking meditation, also called *kinhin.* Kinhin is meditation using movement. Find a quiet place to walk. The place can be a park or spacious room in your house or apartment. If practicing outside find a place far from the "noise pollution" of the city. Walking nearest to nature is recommended because the serene beauty of nature will help you focus on relaxation and bring you closer to your "spirit-mind."

Start the practice of walking meditation by first using the sitting meditation technique found in chapter three for five minutes. After focusing on your breathing while sitting, slowly stand up with eyes slightly lowered. Straighten the back. Make a soft fist with your left hand with left fingers over the left thumb. Adjust the left fist so that the palm is facing and against your chest. Cradle the left fist with the right hand. Position both hands in the middle of your chest just below your heart (at the bottom of your sternum or breast bone). If you'd rather place your arms down at your sides while you walk, that's also fine. You must find your own Zen.

Start with the right foot (some practitioners start with the left foot). Begin walking. Take one step during your inhalation. Take one step during your exhalation. You should be walking to the speed and rhythm of your breathing. Notice the sensations in the heels of your feet as they touch the ground. Be aware of the brief moment your feet are flat on the ground, bend near the toes, and then are flung swiftly through the atmosphere powered by your legs. Take a moment and sense the presence of your legs. Feel the sensations in your legs as you slowly walk. How do your legs feel? Are they tired, asleep, weak, restless, or in pain? Silently observe the feelings in your legs and then let the feelings go. Take a moment and sense the presence of your hara or the spiritual center of your body just below your naval. Notice how your hara rises and falls during the inhalation and exhalation. Focus now on you hands. Be aware of the soft fist you created with the left hand as it is gently cradled by your right hand. Are your arms bent at the elbows and parallel to the ground?

Now notice your breathing. Be aware of the air that flows into your nostrils as you breathe in. Be aware of the air that flows out of your nostrils as you breathe out. Breathe normally without force.

Pay attention to the sounds and sensations of your surroundings. Experience the warm summer breeze as it performs a dance around your face. Experience the radiance of the sun. Does the sunlight gently kiss your cheeks? Be aware of the songs the birds in the trees sing. What thoughts enter your mind as you walk in this manner? Are your thoughts positive? Are your thoughts negative? Accept your thoughts as they appear in your mind and allow them to slowly slip away from your memory, just as the leaves eventually slip away from the trees. Be at total peace. Calm and quiet the mind. Walk this way for 15 minutes.

Impermanence

Zen Buddhism teaches us that joy and happiness cannot be found in material possessions because everything in life is transient or passing soon. Another name for this "passing soon" idea is impermanence. Impermanence represents the flower that blooms with radiant beauty and then slowly withers away, the changing of the seasons, the rising and setting of the sun. Impermanence represents the baby who is born, who grows to childhood, reaches adulthood, achieves old age, and then dies.

The resume also represents impermanence because every time you acquire new work or volunteer experience the life of the resume changes. The original resume you once had withers away. Old information is removed to make room for your new work experience. And if you find that dream job (the one that you can retire from), the resume cycle of being revised or "reborn" to accommodate the requirements of a new employer ceases—just as being "reborn" into *samsara* ceases when one reaches nirvana, and then *parinirvana* (at death).

You will not be able to grasp the concept of impermanence and resume writing if you are trapped in a prison of cluttered thoughts. Every day we bombard ourselves with thoughts that worry and stress us. Sometimes the stress is so bad that a single thought may cause a migraine. We worry about events that occurred in the past. Zen Buddhism teaches us to leave the past in the past. We're haunted by what may happen in the future. Zen Buddhism teaches us to live and focus on the here and now—the present moment.

According to Zen Buddhism, the only place we will find solace in this life is deep within the labyrinth of our mind through meditation. Meditation will calm your body and mind and allow you to appreciate the feeling of being "alive." Life is a miracle within itself. One way life is sustained is through the breath. Zen requires you to focus on the breath during mindfulness meditation. Focusing on the breath helps you gain a deeper appreciation for life because without breath there is no life.

Practicing meditation daily will cleanse you of mental chatter and create a calm and concentrated mind. A calm and concentrated mind is better able to acquire wisdom and enlightenment.

Impermanence represents the flower that blooms with radiant beauty
and then slowly withers away.

Stress Reduction Meditation

Start the practice of stress reduction meditation by first using the sitting meditation technique found in chapter three for ten minutes. After focusing on the breath while in a calm meditative state imagine yourself looking out of an open window. The scene out of the window is of a beautiful blue ocean, and a clear blue sky. In the distant horizon you see a white dove slowly approaching. The dove comes closer and closer until it lands in front of you inside the open window. Once inside the window, see yourself handing the dove a message on a piece of paper. The message describes a stressful thought that is causing you suffering. Now imagine the dove taking this piece of paper in its beak and flying away. See the dove fly farther and farther away over the ocean until it is out of sight. Stare out onto the horizon again. You see that the dove is coming back, but this time without the piece of paper. The dove lands again in front of you inside the open window. Give the dove another message on another piece of paper. The new message is the description of a second stressful thought that is causing you suffering. Imagine the dove taking this new piece of paper in its beak and flying away. See the dove fly farther and farther away over the ocean until it is out of sight.

Repeat this stress reduction meditation until the dove has carried away all of the stressful thoughts in your mind that are causing you suffering.

The dove represents the peace that is going to remain in your heart after the dove has carried all of your stressful thoughts away.

11

Example Resumes

NOTE: The following resume examples represent one page resumes. Book formatting caused some resumes to appear two pages long.

Chronological
Functional
Combination

The Zen question to ask yourself as you write your resume is: "Who am I?"

Buddhist monk practicing sitting meditation.

A Beautiful way to pray for others

is to breathe in their suffering and breathe out your joy.
With each exhalation, feel that you're expelling their pain.
With each inhalation, feel happiness filling the
space created by pulling out their pain.
(Do this as a means to end your own suffering too.)

From The Zen Book, by Daniel Levin

Chronological Resume Outline

Name • Address • Phone Number • Email Address

Work Experience

_____   ____ _ ____

Job Position, Company, City, State

*

*

*

_____   ____ _ ____

Job Position, Company, City, State

*

*

*

_____   ____ _ ____

Job Position, Company, City, State

*

*

*

_____   ____ _ ____

Job Position, Company, City, State

*

*

*

Education

Degree, School, City, State, Year Graduated

Chronological Resume with Cause and Effect

Yolanda Yevette
111 Samsara Way
Dayton, Ohio 45402
937-222-2222
yyevette@emailaddress.com

Achievements

♦ Designed new math comprehension method
♦ Extensive knowledge of trigonometry, geometry, algebra and calculus

Experience

2003-2006
Adult Learning Academy   Dayton, Ohio
Math Tutor
♦ Tutored adult special education students in basic math skills, increasing math grades by one letter grade for 20 students.

2002-2003
The Tutoring Center   Dayton, Ohio
Math Tutor
♦ Taught high school students new study skills for ACT and SAT math tests, convincing 30 students to consider careers in math and math related industries on career outlook survey.

2001-2002
Achievement Center   Dayton, Ohio
Math Tutor
♦ Provided one-on-one math assistance for special needs students. Encouraged an increase in grade point averages for 100 students.

2000-2001
Learning for the Future Academy   Dayton, Ohio
Math Tutor
♦ Created new study method for geometry, algebra and calculus. Reduced math anxiety and increased math test scores by 10%.

Computer Skills: Quicken Deluxe ◆ Excel ◆ PowerPoint ◆ QuickBooks ◆ Microsoft Word

Education

The University of Akron, Coursework Mathematics

Chronological Resume with Objective and Cause and Effect

Connie May 333 Mindfulness Parkway Cincinnati, Ohio
45212 513-111-1234
cmay@emailaddress.com

Objective
Seamstress

Highlights

Experience in wedding dress creation
Baby and toddler clothes designs
Men suit alterations

2005-2006
A-Plus Clothes   Cincinnati, Ohio
Dress Designer

- Designed and created women's suits for interviewing purposes for low-income and homeless citizens, increasing job interview clients at three job placement agencies.

2004-2005
Clothes and Moore   Cincinnati, Ohio
Seamstress

- Altered and adjusted uniforms for nurses, doctors, and maintenance workers, saving hospitals and medical clinics time and money in new uniform orders and costs.

2000-2004
New Era Uniforms   Cincinnati, Ohio
Seamstress

- Sewed from design diagrams and patterns waitress and waiter uniforms for five-star hotel, enhancing the professional look needed for interpersonal communication and receiving "Best Seamstress Award" in 2004.

Related Experience

Other creations and alterations include:

Hats ◆ Gloves ◆ Purses ◆ Maternity Clothes ◆ Military uniform alterations

Education

Continuing education sewing workshop, Cincinnati University, Cincinnati, Ohio, 2000

Chronological Resume with Skills Summary, Objective, and Cause and Effect

Karma Jones
999 Peace Road
Dayton, Ohio 45402
(937) 444-4441
kjones@emailaddress.com

Goal: Motivational Speaker

Motivational speaker with six years experience speaking to high school students and encouraging students to avoid drugs and alcohol by accomplishing goals and staying in school.

Skills

Interpersonal ♦ Speech writing ♦ Public Relations ♦ Communication ♦ Scheduling ♦ Counseling ♦ Mentoring ♦ Training ♦ Organization ♦ Tutoring

Jennings Technical High School, Dayton, Ohio, 2004-2006
Motivational Speaker

♦ Developed seminars designed to teach high school students mentoring skills to encourage younger students to avoid drugs, peer pressure, and alcohol use. Reduced school dropout rate by 50%.

Ewing Aviation High School, Dayton, Ohio, 2002-2004
Motivational Speaker

♦ Counseled troubled teens. Established GED tutoring for school dropout students, maintained good rapport with students' parents, and provided summer job internship placement for students. Increased honor roll membership by 200 students.

Drake County Academy, Dayton, Ohio, 2000-2002
Motivational Speaker

♦ Lectured at student development day seminar encouraging students to enroll in college and stay off drugs. Increased participation in SAT college entrance test practice workshop by 100 students.

Education

University of Dayton Continuing Adult Education, Dayton, Ohio
Excellence in Public Speaking Certificate, 2000

Chronological Resume with Cause and Effect

10 Lovingkindness Plaza
Westlake, Ohio 44145
(440) 888-8881
bkrenshaw@emailaddress.com

Besty May Krenshaw

Awards

Trainer of the Year 2005
Most Improved Trainer 2002

Animal Families 4 Life, London, Ohio   2004-2006
Animal Trainer

• Trained animal shelter canines for special needs clients. Obedience training included: alerting owner when visitors are near front door, alerting owner when phone rings, teaching dogs to stop and go at crosswalks and crosswalk intersections, and retrieving hard-to-reach objects for wheelchair using clients. Canine training caused 100 dogs to be adopted from the program.

Animals-R-Us, St. Clairsville, Ohio   2002-2004
Animal Trainer

• Trained once abandoned canines obedience training including sitting, walking on a leash, and stopping on command. Training caused 30 dogs to be adopted into private homes.

No More Abuse Animal Training, St. Clairsville, Ohio   2001-2002
Animal Trainer

• Conditioned formerly abused and abandoned dogs from animal rescue shelters by: playing special dog development games, walking dogs every day for exercise, sleeping in same room with assigned canines, feeding, bathing and grooming animals. Created people friendly disposition in rescued canines for purpose of adoption.

Chronological Resume with Objective and Cause and Effect

Levin Cavalier
789 Mantra Street
Akron, Ohio 44301
330-789-7899
lcavalier@emailaddress.com

Goal to Achieve: Waitress Supervisor

Waitress
Diner Heaven
Lebanon, Ohio
2004-2006

- Operated cash register and resolved customer meal bills. Balanced accounting records, ordered and stocked kitchen supplies, maintained dinning room area by sweeping floors, busing tables, and vacuuming. Promoted to waitress supervisor for excellent service.

Waitress
The Food Barn
Lebanon, Ohio
2002-2004

- Resolved customer meal disputes by calming customers and alerting manager in a timely manner. Received "Waitress of the Year" recognition for providing prompt service, excellent service, and creating rapport with customers.

Waitress
Momoko's Family Restaurant
Lebanon, Ohio
2000-2002

- Took meal orders from customers, washed dishes, bused tables. Exemplified pleasant and welcoming attitude, creating increase patronage of 20 customers.

Related Skills

- Analytical Skills

- Communication

- Detail Oriented

- Punctuality

- Organization

<u>Education</u>: The University of Akron, Coursework Restaurant Management.

Chronological Resume

John Doe
123 Zen Circle
Akron, Ohio 44304
330-777-4567
jdoe@emailaddress.com

Volunteer Experience

2005-2006
Beautiful View, Incorporated, Medina, Ohio
Landscaper

Planted flowers, grass, small trees, and shrubs around public municipal buildings.

Cared for six public and private gardens aiding growth of 17 varieties of vegetables.

Provided landscape service for three state parks; assisted with grass cutting, weed and critter control, and tree pruning.

2004-2005
Anderson Ground Maintenance Company, Akron, Ohio
Grounds Maintenance Worker

Cleaned city pools by removing pool debris and applying clean water daily.

Removed trash and debris from the tow path area for "Summer Tour of Metro Parks" annual bike riding event.

Planted flowers and shrubs in blighted vacant lots around the city of Akron, Ohio as part of the "Keep Our City Beautiful" campaign.

2002-2004
Brick & Mortar People Incorporated, Akron, Ohio
Bricklayer

Restored historic city roads by replacing cracked or loose bricks.

Applied and replaced bricks for the "Old Stone School" 1800 style historic school building.

Chronological Resume with Objective and Skills Summary

Betty Reed

breed@emailaddress.com

7777 Buddhist Boulevard • Euclid, Ohio 44123 • (216) 777-7777

Objective: Funeral Director Embalmer

Skills Summary

- Six years customer service experience. Phone etiquette certificate 2004.

- Two years embalming experience. Embalming Service Award 2006.

- Computer knowledge includes programming, database creation.

Work History

2004-2006
Apprentice, **Richardson & Richardson Funeral Home**, Euclid, Ohio

- Embalmed, dressed and prepared deceased for viewing.

- Cleaned funeral vehicles, funeral home, and funeral grounds.

- Assisted in calling hour preparation: directed families to viewing area, provided prayer cards and donation envelopes, cleaned funeral home before and after visitor arrival.

2002-2004
Funeral Attendant, **Gordon Funeral Homes**, Canton, Ohio

- Answered phone inquiries concerning funeral arrangements.

- Prepared funeral home for calling hours: cleaned facility, provided payer cards and donation envelopes for visitors, cleared snow from parking lot, and salted walks during winter weather.

2000-2002
Funeral Attendant, **Schmidt-Dhonau Funeral Home**, Reading, Ohio

- Participated in removal service for deceased throughout Cincinnati, Ohio area.

- Participated in light janitorial activities: watered flowers, cleaned offices, and cleaned parking lot in preparation for funeral services.

Education	Associate Degree, Mortuary Science, Cincinnati College of Mortuary Science, 2004

Chronological Resume with Objective

Bill Madison
303 Zazen Avenue
Akron, Ohio 44309
330-991-4567
bmadison@emailaddress.com

Objective
Automotive Engineer

Work Experience

Automotive Technician, **Levar & Sons Motor Company**,
Cleveland, Ohio, 2005-present

* Designed steering wheel airbags for light-duty trucks.

* Invented anti-rust solution for metal door panels.

* Improved car seat cup holders for sport utility vehicles.

Assembler, **General Motors Lordstown Assembly Plant**,
Warren, Ohio, 2003-2005

* Assembled engine components in small car division.

* Installed anti-lock brake systems in compact cars.

* Developed new cushion material in car seat division.

Inspector, **New Cars Inspection Service**, Canton, Ohio, 2002-2003

* Inspected assembly line car components for defects.

* Watched for mistakes in development of new components in chassis room.

Painter, **ABC Paints Company**, Akron, Ohio, 2002

* Invented new paint color for office conference rooms.

* Painted murals for seven municipal and federal buildings.

• Developed anti-flake paint solution for wooden porch furniture.

Special Workshops

Engine Development, Johnson Technical School of Engine Repair, Akron, Ohio
2001

Military Service

US Marine Reserve 1998-2001

Chronological Resume with Skills Summary

Ralph Richards
100 Enso Drive
Akron, Ohio 44308
330-222-4567
rrichards@emailaddress.com

Highlights

Carpenter with five years experience in cabinet making, designing 1880s style furniture, and antique restoration

2005-2006   A&A Construction Company, Orient, Ohio
             Carpenter

- Assembled tables and chairs for three furniture manufacturers using company blueprints.

- Designed kitchen cabinets for low income resident homes.

- Invented new wooden stair design for spiral staircase.

- Restored, refinished, and designed 1880s style furniture for five museums of history.

2003-2005   Build-It-Construction, Medina, Ohio
             Woodworker

- Constructed log cabins for national parks and recreation areas.

- Invented wood preservation solution for historic wooden boats.

- Created wood art sculpture for residential homes and municipal buildings.

- Installed wood paneling in Creeksview Public Library.

2000-2003   John's Artistic Wood Design, Lucasville, Ohio
             Self Employed Wood Art Designer

- Carved religious statues for area churches.

- Created wooden murals for municipal art gallery.

Education   Wood Design Workshop, City Museum of Art, 2000

Chronological Resume with Objective

Jason Simmons

121st Samsara Way, West Mayberry, Ohio 44434, 330.444.4444,
jsimmons@emailaddress.com

Career Goal: Bricklayer

Tool Knowledge: Joint Raker ♦ Brick Lifter ♦ Brick Trowels ♦ Hawks ♦
Gauging Trowels.

WORK HISTORY

Ling Ling Construction Company, Lyndhurst, Ohio, 2004-2006

Bricklayer

Repaired chimneys, fireplaces, and floors for ten model homes.

Used corner lead method to design protective walls for historic mansions.

May Builders Stone Construction, Barberton, Ohio, 2000-2004

Stonemason

Constructed exterior walls from limestone and marble for three municipal
museums.

Worked closely with construction engineers in the interpretation of construction
blueprints.

Education

Stonemason Apprentice Training
May Builders Stone Construction, Barberton, Ohio 2000

Chronological Resume with Objective

Sally Jones
55 Dharma Street
Akron, Ohio 44304
330.555.7777
jsally@emailaddress.com

Career Interest: Construction Laborer

WORK EXPERIENCE

2003-2006
ABC Construction   **Massillon, Ohio**
Laborer

- Applied asphalt on city roads, basketball courts, tennis courts, and play-grounds.

- Installed sewer and drain pipes in neighborhoods.

- Prepared construction sites by removing street debris, asbestos, and lead based paint from targeted facilities.

- Distributed building materials to construction sites.

2000-2003
Richardson Construction   **Lima, Ohio**
Laborer

- Mixed concrete and applied to sidewalks, potholes, and concrete walls.

- Worked closely with engineers, carpenters, stonemasons, and bricklayers.

- Installed traffic barricades around highway construction sites.

Skilled in the following tools

Mortar Mixers, Pavement Breakers, Hydraulic Boring Machines, Jackhammers, and Earth Tampers.

Chronological Resume with Objective

Dontize Rene'
4949 Meditation Street
Cleveland, Ohio 44114
(216) 111-4567
drene@emailadress.com

Objective
Pest Control Technician

Skills: Applicator Manipulation, Fumigant Control, Working in harsh conditions, Communication Skills

Work Experience

2003-2004
Pests-R-Gone Pest Control, Pest Control Technician Canton, Ohio

- Identified pest problems for public and private facilities.

- Repaired structural destruction caused by termites.

- Inspected municipal buildings and homes.

2000-2003
No More Pests, Pest Control Apprentice Akron, Ohio

- Used chemicals to prevent infestation.

- Developed barriers to cut off food supply of pests.

Awards: Excellent Apprentice 2003 ♦ Perfect Attendance 2001 ♦ Technician of the Year 2004.

Education

Applicator Certification, State of Ohio, 2003

Chronological Resume with Objective

David Joanson
1111 Mindfulness Place
Akron, Ohio 44308
(330) 888-8888
djoanson@emailaddress.com

Career Goal: Grounds Maintenance Worker

PROFESSIONAL EXPEREINCE

2005–2006 Groundskeeper, Green Grass Landscaping, Canton, Ohio

Mowed, fertilized, and watered lawns for municipal buildings. Cared for indoor gardens for three public libraries.

2003-2005 Greenskeeper, Tee-for-Me Golf Course, Cleveland, Ohio

Created holes on putting greens. Mowed and watered golf course grounds. Developed sandy putting areas. Repaired tee markers. Designed new benches and canopies.

2001-2003 Groundskeeper, Lakewood Cemetery, Akron, Ohio

Trimmed trees, and pruned bushes around headstones and mausoleums. Maintained memorial garden by planting flowers, mowing, weeding, and removing litter and other debris around headstones.

2000-2001 Groundskeeper, The City Athletic Field, Alliance, Ohio

Vacuumed synthetic turf field to prevent mold and bacteria contamination. Washed and sterilized turf field after each athletic event. Removed litter on and around athletic grounds. Repaired parking lots, benches, fences, and water fountains.

EDUCATION

Kenmore High School

Chronological Resume with Objective

Thomas O'Neal
999 Kinhin Street
Apartment F
Akron, Ohio 44301
toneal@emailaddress.com

Career Focus: Janitor

Special Expertise: Carpet Cleaning ♦ Wallpaper Removal ♦ Drywall ♦ Painting
♦ Floor Restoration

EXPERIENCE

2004-2005
No Dirt Cleaning Services, Columbus, Ohio
Janitor

- Vacuumed, waxed, cleaned floors, and replaced broken and loose tile.

- Removed trash from municipal office cubicles.

2003-2004
Dirt-Be-Gone Cleaning, Canton, Ohio
Cleaning Personnel

- Fixed faucets, painted, cleaned and replenished bathrooms.

- Checked air-conditioning and heating systems.

2000-2003
Get Clean Cleaning Company, Kent, Ohio
Cleaning Personnel

- Mowed lawns, planted flowers, installed fertilizer. Weeded when necessary.

- Dusted and polished furniture.

- Performed minor plumbing repairs.

Awards Employee of the Month, Get Clean Cleaning Company, 2000

Perfect Attendance Award, No Dirt Cleaning Services, 2004-2005

Membership American Janitorial Association

Chronological Resume with Objective

Paul Chang

444 Cosmic Mudra Avenue

Akron, Ohio 44326

(330) 123-5555

pchang@emailaddress.com

Goal to Achieve
Food Service Manager

2004-2006
Jackson & Jacob Meals to Go   **Alliance, Ohio**
Kitchen Manager

• Hired short-order cooks, and monitored new employee training performance.

• Wrote performance evaluations and prepared letters of recommendation for career advancement employees.

• Planned menus and supervised food preparation.

• Participated in preparing lunch and dinner meals.

• Made routine alteration to menu to keep up with food trends.

2001-2004
Sushi One Bar & Grill Restaurant   **Canton, Ohio**
Kitchen Personnel

• Prepared breakfast, lunch, and dinner meals.

• Organized banquets for wedding receptions, high school and college graduations.

• Ordered food spices and ingredients.

2000-2001
Pizza Barn   **Massillon, Ohio**

Prep Cook

- Prepared pizzas, specialty sandwiches, salads, and soups.

- Stocked kitchen area with pizza ingredients and food preparation supplies.

Education

Rene' Richardson School of Culinary Arts, 2001

Chronological Resume with Objective and Skills Summary

Phillip Anderson

1212 Rainbow Lane
Akron, Ohio 44320
330-543-2100
panderson@emailaddress.com

Professional Career Interest
Sheet Metal Worker

Sheet Metal Worker with five years experience in metal manipulation and construction, balancing, adjusting, and testing air conditioning and ventilation systems

EXPERIENCE	2004-2006	**Thompson Metal Works Akron, Ohio** Sheet Metal Worker Assistant

- Operated computerized metalworking equipment used for cutting and shaping metal material.

- Developed metal components for heating, air conditioning duct systems, and ventilation systems.

	2003-2004	**Simone's Metal Works Akron, Ohio** Metal Worker Assistant

- Analyzed blueprint specifications and layout plans before creating finished products.

- Manipulated computer-controlled saws, presses, and lasers.

- Repaired metal stamping machinery.

2001-2003   **Peterson Machines Akron, Ohio**
               Metal Worker Assistant

               • Used calipers and micrometers to check
                 machine parts for accuracy.

               • Connected sheet metal parts with rivets, sol-
                 der, welds, and sheet metal drive clips.

               • Tested and adjusted air conditioning systems.

EDUCATION   Peterson Machines, Apprentice, 2003

                HVAC License, State of Ohio, 2000

Chronological Resume with Objective

Betty Brown
5551 Visualize Street
Akron, Ohio 44301
330-123-1231
bbrown@emailaddress.com

Professional Focus
Hazardous Material Removal

EXPERIENCE

2004-present
Terrace Chemical Removal   **Medina, Ohio**
Asbestos and Lead Abatement Worker

- Removed asbestos from nine municipal buildings and schools.

- Participated in crew of 20 in the removal of lead-based paint from low-income houses in the Akron, Canton, and Medina areas.

- Stripped hazardous material from buildings scheduled to be demolished.

2002-2004
Disposal-R-US   **Akron, Ohio**
Cleaning Personnel

- Cleaned and removed dangerous debris from buildings scheduled to be renovated.

- Used high-pressure water sprayers and sandblasters to remove lead from large buildings.

- Measured construction site for air quality for protection and safety of coworkers.

2000-2002
Safety Hazards Disposal Company   **Lakemore, Ohio**
Decontamination Technician

- Removed radioactive material from nuclear power plants, and prepared material for transportation and disposal.

LICENSE

Asbestos Abatement and Lead Abatement License, State of Ohio, 2002

Chronological Resume with Objective

Allison Fredrickson
999 Healing Place
Akron, Ohio 44308
(330) 456-7890
afredrickson@emailaddress.com

Career Scope: Library Technician

<u>WORK EXPERIENCE</u>

2005-2006
Women's History Public Library, Library Clerk, **Columbus, Ohio**

• Organized newspaper and magazine subscriptions.

• Bound and preserved historic documents.

• Processed interlibrary loan requests.

2003-2005
The Historic Museum Public Library, Library Assistant, **Cincinnati, Ohio**

• Processed new library material by applying Library of Congress number, protective covering, and other identifying information.

• Prepared supply invoice, ordered and maintained library supplies.

• Instructed patrons on computer database.

• Maintained audiovisual equipment including projectors, DVD players, CD players, Kurzweil Systems, and JAWS Screen Readers.

2000-2003
Aviation Public Library, Library Assistant, **Cleveland, Ohio**

• Shelved library material, and restocked supplies.

• Helped patrons with microfilm and microfiche machines.

• Designed library display case showcasing new books.

Computer Skills:

Microsoft Word, Excel, PowerPoint, Outlook, Internet Searching

<u>EDUCATION</u>

The University of Akron, Coursework, History, Akron, Ohio

Chronological Resume with Objective

Fred Freemason   ffreemason@emailaddress.com
24701 Suffering Street
Barberton, Ohio 44203
330-460-6433

Objective: Bookkeeper

2003-2006
Wilson Copy Center   **Medina, Ohio**
Timekeeper Clerk

- Worked in human resource department proofreading and checking employee timecards for errors.

- Analyzed computer reports. Distributed paychecks. Performed clerical duties.

2000-2003
Thompson Copy Center   **Barberton, Ohio**
Payroll Clerk

- Performed payroll calculations by subtracting Federal and State taxes, allotments, and retirement contributions.

- Counted and recorded money from photocopy machines.

Computer Skills
- Microsoft Word • Access • HTML
- PowerPoint • Excel • QuickBooks software

Additional Expertise: Payroll processing ♦ Tax Law ♦ Accounting procedures ♦ Receipt balancing ♦ Invoice preparation ♦ Automated timekeeping systems.

Awards: Employee of the month 2000, Best Clerk 2003, Excellent Employee 2004.

Certification
Certified Bookkeeper, State of Ohio, 2000

Associations
American Institute of Professional Bookkeepers

Chronological Resume with Objective

Freda Jones
3222 Craving Circle
Akron, Ohio 44308
330-456-7890
fjones@emailaddress.com

Career Scope
Animal Care Worker

Maple Valley Animal Care Akron, Ohio 2006-present

Kennel Attendant Provided basic care for animals. Exercised animals, prepared food and water, and cleaned cages.

Archwood Animal Grooming, Canton, Ohio 2004-2006

Animal Groomer Maintained grooming care. Bathed animals, dispensed medicines, trimmed nails, cut and shampooed fur.

My Favorite Paws Pet Supplies, Barberton, Ohio 2002-2004

Customer Service Sold pet supplies. Restocked shelves, operated cash register, priced merchandise, and maintained inventory of pet supplies.

Frederickson Animal Care Center, Alliance, Ohio 2000-2002

Animal Assistant Assisted with animal breeding, and obedience training.

Cared for stray and abandon baby animals. Prepared animals for adoption by getting them used to human contact.

Associations

The American Boarding Kennels Association

Functional Resume Outline

Name ♦ Address ♦ Phone Number ♦ Email Address

Accomplishments

_____

Skill Area

*

*

*

_____

Skill Area

*

*

*

_____

Skill Area

*

*

*

Work Experience

_____   _____—_____

Job Position, Company, City, State

_____   _____—_____

Job Position, Company, City, State

_____   _____—_____

Job Position, Company, City, State

Education

Degree, School, City, State, Year Graduated

Functional Resume with Objective

Mai Chang
242 Attachment Lane
Akron, Ohio 44304
(330) 333-12345
mchang@emailaddress.com

Objective: Medical Assistant

Communication

- Answered patient inquiries over the phone.

- Greeted new and existing patients in doctor's office.

- Explained treatment procedures to new and existing patients.

- Telephoned prescriptions to area pharmacies and maintained prescription records.

Organization

- Scheduled medical appointments.

- Prepared insurance forms.

- Maintained and filed medical records.

- Arranged laboratory tests.

Mathematical

- Assisted with medical billing and bookkeeping procedures.

Work Experience

Samson Medical Clinic, Canton, Ohio, 2002-2005

Education

Medical Assisting Certificate
Momoko Community College, Medina, Ohio 2002

Additional Experience: Vital sign monitoring ◆ Medicine administration ◆ Specimen collection ◆ Blood drawing experience.

Functional Resume

Ling Ling Lee
4 Noble Truths Street
Akron, Ohio 44309
330-333-3337
llee@emailaddress.com

Skills and Accomplishments

Communication

- Created career workshops for graduating GED students.
- Taught class on public speaking and presentations.
- Developed job and career search programs for current job seekers.

Training

- Taught library students the elements of the Dewey Decimal System.
- Created workshop to help adult learners with basic writing skills.
- Tutored students in resume and cover letter writing.

Management

- Organized maintenance crew of 30 workers.
- Supervised 100 landscape employees for maintenance of municipal building lawns.
- Designed and maintained daily work schedules for three janitorial companies.

Work Experience

Cardwell Learning Company, Fairlawn, Ohio, 2003-2006
Frederickson & Mann Education Foundation, Canton, Ohio 2001-2003
The Education Group, Westlake, Ohio 2000-2001
Johnson Maintenance Company Euclid, Ohio 2000

Education

Coursework in English, The University of Akron, Akron, Ohio

Functional Resume with Skills Summary
and Cause and Effect

Jim Chun   232 Eightfold Path, Akron, Ohio 44208 (330)555-4555
jchun@emailaddress.com

Summary of Experience

• Five years tow motor operation experience.

• Factory skills include three years machine press operation.

• Experience in woodworking and bricklaying participating in 20 school construction projects.

Skills and Achievements

Creativity

• Created wooden art pieces for 15 public libraries increasing attendance by 20 extra customers a day.

• Designed wooden playground equipment for four municipal preschools providing child-safe areas to play in.

Organization

• Rearranged stock room providing easy access to factory machine merchandise.

• Redesigned factory inventory room removing hidden safety hazards.

Machine Knowledge: Boring Machine ♦ Turning Machine ♦ Milling Machine ♦ Lay and Drilling Machines.

Work Experience

OPUS Machine Company 2005-present
F4u4 Corsair Machine Shop 2003-2005
EFG Incorporated 2000-2003

Special   Employee of the Year, OPUS Machine Company, 2006
Award

Education   Machine Shop Workshop, F4uf Corsair Machine Shop, Canton, Ohio 2003
Press Operator Training, EFG Incorporated, Medina, Ohio 2000

Functional Resume with Cause and Effect

Eric Peoples

333 Buddha-Nature Street • Akron, Ohio 44302 • 330.444.2222
epeoples@emailaddress.com

Computer Skills

Adobe InDesign
Adobe PhotoDelux
Adobe Illustrator

Cartoonist

Designed and published political cartoons for book, "Attack of the Political Cartoon Makers," causing an increase in book sales in 2006.

Photographer

Photographed nature scenes for city of Akron, Ohio's "Clean Up Our City" campaign focusing on blighted areas made beautiful by program volunteers, increasing visitors to selected areas by 10%.

Graphic Artist

Developed coloring and activity book for children of participants of Cuyahoga Valley National Park's "Walking Society Summer Fun" activity, creating 100 additional participating children in 2004.

Free-Lance Work Experience

Association of American Cartoonists, 2006
City of Akron Recreation Bureau, 2005
Cuyahoga Valley National Park, 2004

Education

BA, Graphic Design, The University of Akron, 2004

Functional Resume

Sam Jones
1214 Impermanence Boulevard
Richfield, Ohio 44286
330-333-4444
sjones@emailaddress.com

Objective: Assembler, Fabricator

Tool Knowledge: Floor Lift ♦ Load Lifter ♦ Vertical Band Saw ♦ Radial Arm Drill

Skills

Automobile Assembly
Assembled automobile engine parts for compact cars.

Airplane Assembly
Reconstructed and installed small airplane engine parts for commercial cargo planes.

Electronic Assembly
Worked with team of 10 assemblers in development of computer components.

Metal Fabricator
Measured, fitted, and cut metal parts according to detailed blueprints.

Experience

General Motors Lordstown Assembly Plant, Warren, Ohio 2003-present
Computer World, Alliance, Ohio 2002
Machines & More, Akron, Ohio 2001
Airplanes & More, Akron, Ohio 2000

Military Experience

Marine Reserve 1999-2001

Combination Resume Outline

Name ♦ Address ♦ Phone Number ♦ Email Address

Accomplishments

_____

Skill Area

*

*

*

_____

Skill Area

*

*

*

_____

Skill Area

*

*

*

Work Experience

_____   _____—_____

Job Position, Company, City, State

*

*

*

_____   _____—_____

Job Position, Company, City, State

*

*

*

Education

_____

Degree, School, City, State, Year Graduated

Combination Resume with Cause and Effect

Allison Richardson
1914 No Self Street
Akron, Ohio 44301
330-221-4567
arichardson@emailaddress.com

Skills and Accomplishments

Leadership

- Named primary organizer of corporate research programs.
- Expanded survey research team from 10 to 100 employees.
- Selected focus groups for library levy renewal campaign.

Organization

- Designed customer satisfaction surveys for major corporations.
- Created mall surveys to assess consumer buying patterns.
- Prepared statistical reports and submitted to clients.

Research

- Analyzed survey data, influencing fiscal decisions for two companies.
- Provided research data, improving customer satisfaction for major client.

Work Experience

2005-2006
Connie May Research Incorporated, Survey Researcher, Akron, Ohio

- Organized survey projects, improving statistical analysis.
- Trained 20 employees on research gathering computer database, increasing research retrieval by 50%.
- Developed new market research procedure for two companies, cutting research gathering time by one hour.

Combination Resume with Skills Summary and Cause and Effect

Mark Anderson

123 Right Concentration Street • Medina, Ohio 44256 • (330) 456-7890
manderson@emailaddress.com

Librarian with five years experience in reference management, Web page creation, and computer training

Qualifications	Communication

- Answered reference questions which aided patrons in navigation of internet resources.

- Compiled information booklets containing bibliographies to help students find useful reference sources.

- Presented resume workshops providing information to help patrons with their resume and cover letters.

- Compiled databases and retrieval systems to help patrons find business and government related information.

Leadership

- Mentored 11 student interns teaching them to analyze users' needs to determine appropriate material to order and display.

- Voted Staff Association President overseeing activities such as fund-raising, staff parties, bake sales, and special speaker events.

Experience   2001-present
                        Anderson Public Library, Warren, Ohio
                        Librarian

                        • Designed employment workshops for seniors, resulting
in an increase in circulation of job search books by 50%.

<u>Quote from 2006 Employee Evaluation</u>: "Mark Anderson is an excellent, hardworking, punctual, dependable, and skilled asset to the library organization."

                    1985-2001
                        Anderson Public Library, Warren, Ohio
                        Public Service Assistant

                        • Ordered circulation supplies. Operated library switchboard. Answered phone inquiries concerning patron records. Operated cash register and recorded fines.

Computer Skills: Microsoft Word ♦ PowerPoint ♦ Excel ♦ Internet Searching ♦ HTML/JavaScript ♦ Westlaw ♦ Database Creation.

Education   MLS, Kent State University, Kent, Ohio 2001

Combination Resume with Objective and Cause and Effect

Fred Smith

494 Right Effort Avenue ● Canton, Ohio 44404 ● 330.443.4222

Objective   Heavy equipment mechanic

Creativity   Invented and designed three fuel efficient ethanol powered engine styles, one of which debuted at "Invention at the Races" mini-car racing event in 2003.

Training   Developed workshop on minor emergency car engine repair for "Women's Health Day" expo providing better understanding of car mechanics.

Work Experience

Pleasant Municipal Roads Department, Pleasant, Ohio 2002-2004
Mechanical Assistant

• Repaired and operated steamroller engines used in the maintenance of city roads. Used voltmeters and ohmmeters to check electrical systems.

• Carried out weekly maintenance checks on diesel engines, brake, fuel, suspension and transmission systems, and excavator equipment.

• Assisted cleaning and clearing highway in preparation of road damage repair.

Richardson's Garage, Akron, Ohio 2000-2002
Mechanic

• Repaired farm equipment including tractor motors, truck engines, wood chippers and chainsaws.

• Refurbished antique farm tractor engines and tractor frames for "Museum of Early Farm Devices."

• Repaired hydraulics, transmission, and electrical systems for bulldozers and railcars.

Education

Brainbridge Technical School for Heavy Equipment Operators
Heavy Equipment Technician, 2000

Combination Resume with Objective and Cause and Effect

Barry Lyons
555 Right Speech Boulevard
Cuyahoga Falls, Ohio 44320
330-456-7890
blyons@emailaddress.com

OBJECTIVE	**Machinist**
Listening Skills	Detected problems in precision machine tools by listening for irregular sounds. Once problems were detected, developed testing measures to solve problems.
Computer Literacy	Adjusted settings and calibrated computer numerically controlled machines, increasing machine productivity by one hour.
Detail Oriented	Worked with computer control programs to see how metal material would be shaped and cut. Cut and shaped material from special specifications resulting in finished products.
EXPERIENCE 2004-2006 Johnson Machine Shop Canton, Ohio	
Assistant Machinist	Fixed and designed new parts for existing machine and warehouse equipment, increasing production time by 10%.
TOOL EXPERTISE:	Precision Parallels ♦ Micrometers ♦ Digital Calipers ♦ Protractor ♦ Height Gages ♦ Test Indicators.
EDUCATION	Madison Vocational School, Machine Shop Training Akron, Ohio 2003

12

The Interview

Once the employer accepts your resume and calls you in for an interview the most challenging question you may encounter is:

Why do you have a three year gap in work history?

The above question may cause you suffering because you are going to start to worry about how the employer will accept you and perceive you with a criminal record. Accept those feelings for what they are and let them go leaving only an empty space. Zen teaches us to leave the past in the past and dwell on the present moment—the here and now. Zen also teaches us to show compassion no matter what the situation. Silently send the interviewer lovingkindness so that you do not see the interviewer as someone to fear, but you see the interviewer as a friend. In Zen Buddhism, we are all part of the universe. We are all interconnected. We are all one. To relieve interview stress, you can also imagine that the employer was once your brother or sister, or your father or mother in another lifetime. Next, focus on how you will answer the present question. Make the answer to this question brief and to the point. Do not ramble on and on about your conviction. Do not provide any more information than was asked. Your answer may go something like this:

1. I was convicted of (make the answer very brief, i.e., a drug related conviction).

2. I spent (reveal the time frame, i.e., three years incarcerated).

3. I have learned from my mistakes and have rehabilitated my life for the better by (provide evidence, i.e., completing vocational training).

At this point the employer may ask you to give examples of how you have taken responsibility for your actions. Take the opportunity to discuss how you turned your life around. Discuss accomplishment after accomplishment:

A. I have taken responsibility for my actions by educating myself and receiving my GED.

B. I have taken courses to better myself including workshops in engine repair.

C. I have acquired skills in carpentry and building maintenance.

D. I was a model citizen and helped other inmates by tutoring them in reading and writing skills.

E. I participated in several volunteer activities including training dogs for special needs people.

Another challenging question the employer may ask is:

Why should I hire someone with a criminal record?

Once again show the employer you have changed your way of thinking and acting, and you took the necessary steps to live and act accordingly. You answer may go something like this:

My past is no longer a part of me and is no indication of my present and future actions. Incarceration has helped me become a qualified person because I have turned my "prison time" into "quality time." I have taken advantage of all the mechanical workshops, and educational workshops offered. I have participated in training programs which provided me a working knowledge of the machine shop trade. I am now determined, motivated, encouraged, and committed to be a hard-working, productive member of society for the betterment of society. In your company's mission statement it says that you provide "quality customer service." With my five years of training and experience in customer relations, I have the skills you are looking for to enhance your "quality customer service."

Visuals

Visuals work well in interviews. If you took a writing course and received a certificate of completion, you can use that visual in the interview as an example of your excellent writing skills. If you wrote articles for the prison newspaper, for instance, a sample of your newspaper article is a powerful tool. Two or three of your best visuals are excellent examples of evidence to back up your work experience. Show no more than three visuals. You do not want to overwhelm the employer.

Examples of visuals include:

1. Letters of recommendation from past employers.

2. Certificates of completion from educational workshops.

3. Samples of your work, i.e., writing sample (especially one that was published).

4. A good quality photo of a completed construction, woodworking, or art project you participated in while in prison (related to employment).

5. Awards from past jobs like an "employee of the month" award, or "good attendance" award (to show that you are punctual, and a good worker).

6. Employee evaluation from a past employer highlighting an excellent evaluation of you.

Common Interview Questions

Here are some common interview questions an employer might ask. Practice the answers to these questions with a friend.

1. Tell me about yourself?

2. Why did you apply for this position?

3. Why should I hire you?

4. What skills do you have that prepares you for this job?

5. What do you know about our company?

6. What can you contribute to this company?

7. What kind of tools or machines can you operate?

8. How do you handle stressful situations?

9. What are your goals for the next five years?

10. What are your strengths/weaknesses?

Interview Don'ts

Do not …

1. Arrive late.

2. Dress poorly.

3. Speak poorly. Do not use street language or slang.

4. Give yes or no answers. Answer the questions completely. Give examples when necessary.

5. Have poor hygiene.

6. Lie. Lies will catch up to you sooner or later.

7. Look away from the interviewer. Maintain eye contact during the interview.

8. Talk too much when explaining something.

9. Sound negative. Always accentuate the positive in an interview, never the negative. Never talk about past employers in a negative way.

10. Talk about salary and benefits in the beginning of the interview.

Salary

Allow the employer to mention the salary and benefit package first, unless the employer asks you about your salary requirements upfront. If this is the case, as mentioned earlier in chapter five in the "Resume Writing Checklist," if the employer asks you about salary you can say salary is negotiable.

Interview Dos

1. Prepare for the interview. Find out all you can about the company.

2. Always thank the employer for her time at the end of the interview.

3. Shake hands with the employer after the interview.

4. Ask the employer if you can call within a week to inquire about your status.

Always Ask the Employer Questions after the Interview

It is very important to ask the employer questions after the interview. Employers appreciate an eager potential employee and asking the right questions shows the employer you are interested in the job. At the end of the interview expect the employer to ask:

Do you have any questions for me?

Here are four examples to consider:

1. What qualities do you expect out of employees which made your company "Number one in car sales in 2006?" (Research the company and quote an accomplishment).

2. Does your company promote or support additional training or education programs related to the job? (Tell the employer you are eager to learn as much as you can on the job for the betterment of the job and would be willing to participate in any additional educational programs).

3. How does your company motivate people to work to their highest potential? (Tell the employer you have what it takes to get the job done, give examples).

4. If I were hired, what are the goals you'd expect me to accomplish in the first 90 days? (Tell the employer you have the necessary skills to accomplish those goals, give examples).

Brave
Japanese Kanji
Each job interview involves bravery.

Thank You Letter

After the interview immediately mail a typed thank you letter. The envelope you send the letter in should also have typed addresses on it. No handwritten envelopes please. The letter should reach the employer within a few days.

Thank the employer for taking the time to interview you. Discuss how your work experience matches the goals and requirements of the company. Conclude the letter by reminding the employer that you will be contacting the employer concerning your status. Don't forget to sign your name within the spaces between "Sincerely" and your typed name.

Example Thank You Letter

John Doe
100 Appleberry Street
Akron, Ohio 44301
330-221-4567
jdoe@emailaddress.com

June 20, 2006

Alfred Johnson
Human Resource Director
Brothers Heavy Equipment Company
102 Everett Road
Akron, Ohio 44333

Dear Mr. Johnson:

Thank you for the chance to interview for the heavy equipment operator position. I appreciate your interest in my experience and skills.

I believe that my five years as a heavy equipment assistant operator as well as a motor repair mechanic prepared me for the requirements you are looking for.

I'm ready, motivated, and determined to be an asset to your company. I will call you concerning my status next week.

Sincerely,

John Doe

13

Job Search Tips

The number one way to locate employment is through "networking." Networking simply means asking your friends, family, teachers, barber, beautician, postman, pastor, and neighbor about information on current job openings. The networking technique can also be used when contacting the business or trade organization related to the industry you want to work for. You can also request permission to go to the organization's meetings or workshops to talk to members. Two informative association resources include "Columbia Books' National Trade and Professional Associations of the United States," and "Thompson Gale's Encyclopedia of Associations." Both association resources not only provide a brief description of the organizations but provide the names, addresses, phone numbers, Web sites and contact information associated with the organizations. Many association Web sites provide links where you can browse for jobs and apply directly for positions.

Cold Calling

Cold calling or calling the company you want to work for directly is another way to find employment. Ask to be connected to the human resource department and inquire if they are accepting applications or hiring. Check out the company's Web site for employment information. Remember the name of the hiring manager or human resource director after you call so that you can list their name in your cover letter.

Newspaper Ads

Don't answer job ads in the local paper that do not provide enough information about the position, the company, or contact information. In addition to information about the position, I like to see ads with at least five contacts: name of company, address, phone number, fax number, and email address. Beware. Some job ads are scams. A job ad with only an email address, or only a PO Box number, and no information about the position should send up red flags. Also, do not send money to any "work-at-home" ads.

Internet

Do not spend all of your job search time posting your resume on job posting sites or job boards on the Internet. You will be disappointed. Only a small number of job-seekers find jobs online. If you want to post your resume online go directly to a company's Web site. Use job posting sites to do industry research, find job descriptions, acquire salary information, or locate job search tips.

Research Important Facts about the Company

Once you find a company and are able to acquire an interview do research on the company. Write down important facts about the company and present your findings during the interview. It doesn't hurt to take some notes about the company to the interview. A good starting place to find company background information is the company's Web site or contact the business and government section of your local library.

14

Healing Meditation

You cannot write a resume if you are feeling under the weather. Begin healing meditation by first concentrating on the breath using the sitting meditation described in chapter three for ten minutes. After ten minutes of concentrating on the breath say a phrase to yourself to begin the healing session:

Breathe in, *"I heal myself,"* breathe out, *"I'm healthy."*

In Tibetan Buddhist practice, healing the mind and body is performed using mental images of light, rainbow colors, and earth elements—water, fire, wind, space and air. One technique is to imagine a ball of light emitting healing rays that engulf and heal your whole body, or you can visualize light raining down on you. Since the sound of rain is calming to me, when I meditate on healing, I like to use the imagery of a cloud filled with healing droplets of warm light.

Imagine you have, hovering over you, a cloud of white healing light. The cloud is large enough to fit around the circumference of your body.

Just as a MRI (Magnetic Resonance Imaging) machine scans the body for imperfections, so too does the essence of your cloud of light, except that the rain from your cloud permeates, finds, dissolves, and washes any hidden imperfections that may cause harm to your body. In Tibetan Buddhist practice if you have an aliment that feels cold, imagine the healing light as a warm sensation melting the cold affliction in that area of the body. If you have an aliment that feels hot, imagine the healing light as a cool sensation extinguishing the burning feeling in that area of the body.

In your mind, place the cloud of healing energy at the top of your head (you are now physically under the cloud). See the cloud raining down healing illuminated raindrops on you. Feel the droplets permeating your head, eyes, ears, nose, and throat, slowly permeating your whole body. Relax every part of the body that the rain's light permeates. Imagine your rain's light energy finding and eliminating impurities and toxins hiding in your body. As the droplets slowly move down the length of your body, feel the rain's light soaking up all bad cells (free radicals) leaving only good healthy cells in their place. See your cells as healthy and clean. Sense the rain's light energy slowly moving over the chest area. Watch in your mind's eye the warm healing power absorbing, melting, and washing away any plaque hiding in the veins so that blood can easily flow to and from the heart. See the veins as clear and free of debris. Now sense the powerful droplets clearing away harmful pollutants trapped in the lungs. We are constantly breathing in and bombarded by harmful pollutants from vehicle exhausts, factory emissions, and secondhand smoke. See the lungs as strong and clear of pollutants. The rain slowly moves along your arms and hands creating strength and releasing healing power in the muscles. Feel the healing light dripping down to the stomach and intestinal area. Physically feel the rain's light energy depositing healing power to help with the processing of food. The healing rain now permeates the thigh area. See the powerful light droplets strengthening the muscles in the thighs allowing you to walk with vigor, vitality, and for longer periods of time. The light droplets are now moving into your knees releasing healing to strengthen the cartilage within the knees. Feel the illuminated rain now moving to the feet providing the feet the support and energy needed for walking, dancing, and running marathons while the rain gently releases healthy doses of healing light along the way. After the rain of light touches the feet observe the droplets of healing energy leaving the body and going into the ground. Sense that the droplets of light deposited healing fuel in every part of your body illuminating you with healing light. This concludes the healing exercise.

Remember to allow the healing droplets of light to permeate and heal the whole body. In addition, as light droplets permeates your body be completely aware or "mindful" of the drenched area of the body. In other words, try to feel-sense-touch-see the "life" in the permeated body part, even down to the smallest vein and the tiny cells in your body. Being "aware" of every part of your body that the droplets absorb is Zen. Whichever healing method you use, always find your own Zen.

Remain in sitting meditation focusing on the breath for a few more minutes before you open your eyes. Allows your thoughts to come and go leaving only an empty space.

Practice this healing meditation every day on yourself, and as an expression of lovingkindness toward a person you know who is sick and suffering. Begin the meditation session again, remove the words "I'm" and "myself" from the meditation phrase you recited in the beginning of the exercise and include the name of a sick person you know. See the healing cloud of light over the sick person. Now begin to breathe:

Breathe in, *"I heal mother,"* breathe out, *"mother's healthy."*

Zen Thoughts: Another way to heal.

Another way to heal others is to always see yourself as the other person because in Zen there is no separate self. According to Zen, we are all part of the universe. We are all one. By seeing yourself as the other person you should always send lovingkindness to that person as a reflection of what you want for yourself.

The next time you enter a room full of people, or are involved in any group setting with people, silently send lovingkindness to all the people involved so that positive energy can permeate the room. You'll be surprised by the results. Positive energy generates happiness. Happiness causes the brain to secrete chemicals called endorphins. Endorphins relieve pain and make the body feel good, and a happy body is usually a healthy body.

Breathe. Breathe again.

Breathe in acceptance, breathe out criticism. Breathe.
Breathe again. Breathe in love, breathe out hatred. Breathe.
Breathe again. Breathe in whatever you want, and breathe
out whatever no longer serves you.

From The Zen Book, by Daniel Levin

Another Form of Meditation: Visualization

Now that you understand some of the principles of Zen and have practiced Zen meditation before reading each chapter of this book, there is another form of meditation that may add depth and direction to your resume experience—visualization (the technique used in the healing and stress reduction meditation). Visualization is the process of creating pictures in your mind. The pictures you create in your mind are not the scenes of "wanting" something to happen. According to Zen Buddhism, "wanting" causes suffering. The pictures you create in your mind through visualization are scenes that are happening to you now. In other words, start by following the sitting meditation technique in chapter three for ten minutes then imagine you are working now (today) in the job you seek. You are operating heavy equipment—your training is through an apprenticeship. You are typing legal documents as a paralegal secretary. You are preserving historical artifacts in the Museum of Natural History. Practice visualization for five or ten minutes.

Zen Buddhism teaches us to focus and concentrate on the present. The process of visualization is the process of creating a mental picture as if it is happening to you in the present. The mental picture you create in your mind is karma which one day will transform itself into reality. Why does the mental picture you create in your mind eventually become real? According to the laws of karma where there is an action in the universe a reaction soon follows. Remember, in Zen, karma is neither good nor bad; it is just a reaction to an action. Thought is also an action that will generate a reaction. Thought is always trying to manifest itself into reality. In other words, your thoughts are fighting to get out of the prison of you head and become real. This is why the Eightfold Path says to have Right Thought because your thoughts affect your world and the world around you, and to have Right Speech because what you say affects your world and the world around you.

By concentrating and directing a thought on one goal, the strength of that thought is magnified tenfold. The same concept is seen in prayer. Studies have shown that sick people who are prayed for tend to heal faster. Prayer, like meditation and visualization, is a concentrated action (cause) focused toward one goal (effect).

Visualization is a powerful tool made up of natural laws found in the universe. The natural laws may be explained by discoveries in quantum physics that reveal that the universe is made up of particles (electrons, protons, etc.) that are some-how interconnected (*David Bohm's quantum potential and implicate order*). The universe is an ever changing entity made up of a force that is a part of everything and affects everything. A thought is made up of that force.

The universal laws governing the universe are the same laws Buddha understood thousands of years ago when he said nothing is permanent (static), everything is transient (dynamic), your actions and thoughts (karma), affect the universe (cause and effect), and we are all interdependent on and a part of one another (physics).

See yourself in the here and now working at your new job every day and every night. Never give up on this concentrated thought until you reach your goal. Visualization is a force we all possess and it is only when you repeat this thought over and over will the power of your mental energy manifest itself into reality.

Appendix: A
Zen Definitions

Buddha—The Enlightened One. Siddhartha Gautama. An ordinary man in India who left his wealth and privilege and discovered a pathway to the end of suffering.

Cosmic Mudra—Hand position in sitting meditation with the dominate hand cupping or below the non-dominate hand. The tips of the thumbs are lightly touching forming an oval.

Eightfold Path—Right Understanding. Right Thought. Right Speech. Right Action. Right Livelihood. Right Effort. Right Mindfulness. Right Concentration.

Impermanence—The concept of everything in life passing soon. Our passing existence on this earth. Impermanence represents the flower that blooms with radiant beauty and then slowly withers away, the changing of the seasons, the rising and setting of the sun. Impermanence represents the baby who is born, who grows to childhood, reaches adulthood, achieves old age, and then dies. The resume also represents impermanence because every time you acquire new work or volunteer experience the life of the resume changes. The original resume you once had withers away.

Dhammapada—Buddhist scripture made up of 423 verses compiled into a book after the Buddha's death.

Dharma—The teachings of Buddhism.

Enlightenment—An understanding of our place in the universe. Giving up of desires and attachments. Total enlightenment is the complete end of suffering and rebirth called *parinirvana*.

Enso—Zen symbol that represents the idea that everything in life is in constant motion. The enso also represents enlightenment.

Four Noble Truths—Life includes suffering. Suffering is caused by craving and attachments. Suffering can be overcome. Suffering can be overcome by following the Eightfold Path.

Hara—Spiritual center of the body. The *hara* is located two inches below the naval.

Karma—Cause and effect. Our actions. According to the law of karma, your actions in this life affect the quality of your next life. Any action taken in the universe causes a reaction in the universe. In Zen, karma is neither good nor bad; it's just a reaction to an action.

Kanji—(Seen throughout the book) Japanese character writing which number in the thousands. Each Kanji character represents a different idea.

Kinhin—Zen walking meditation.

Lotus Position—Cross-legged meditation position practiced on a special cushion on the floor.

Mantra—Mantras are phrases or syllables Buddhists use to calm the mind and heal the body. The most recognized mantra is, "Om mani padme hum," which refers to Buddha, his truth, compassion, and blessings.

Metta—Universal love.

Metta Sutta or Sutra—The Buddhist scripture that pertains to universal love.

Mindfulness—Being aware or mindful of the present moment by using the breath.

Nirvana—The state of giving up desire and attachment.

Oneness—Not attaching labels or expectations to experiences, but accepting experiences for what they are. Oneness is the acknowledgement of all feelings and sensations (whether good or bad) and allowing those feelings and sensations to pass away leaving only an empty space.

Samsara—The foundation of Buddhist belief encompasses the idea of continuous life cycles also called samsara, or the endless cycle of birth and rebirth. Another way to interpret samsara is to say our present life on earth as a result of the endless process of birth and rebirth. In other words, when a person dies life begins anew on earth. Suffering also begins anew on earth. The process of birth and rebirth stops when a person gives up constant desire and attachment and reaches total enlightenment (the complete end of suffering and rebirth) called *parinirvana*. Zen Buddhists consider rebirth as just another state of being. In Zen belief, to be reborn is to become one with all things.

Sutta or Sutra—Buddhist scripture.

Visualization—A form of meditation in which you create pictures in your mind. The mental picture you create in your mind is karma (cause) which one day may transform itself into reality (effect).

Walking Meditation—Meditation using movement.

Zazen—Sitting meditation. Zazen can be practiced in a chair or while in the cross-legged lotus position.

Zen—The word for "meditation" in Japanese. Zen is a pathway to living in the present moment with the road map found in the mind. Zen is the mechanism used to tap into the true nature (Buddha-nature) of the mind.

Zen Buddhism—A branch of Buddhism that dates back to Buddha's initial teachings. Zen sprang from Mahayana Buddhism which is a form of Buddhism that does not rely on dogma or ritual practice. In Zen, meditation is the key. *The Zen of Resume Writing* will help you "awaken" wisdom, compassion, awareness, and enlightenment by providing Zen meditations. Zen is believed to have been brought to the Far East by an Indian master by the name of Bodhidharma.

Appendix: B
Resume Definitions

Action Verbs—Words that carry the action in a sentence. In resume writing you begin sentences in the work experience section with action verbs.

Cause and Effect Relationship—Results of your work duties. In other words, what did you do to make your job better?

Combination Resume—Both the functional and chronological resumes in one resume. The top half of the combination resume is a functional resume, while the bottom half is a chronological resume.

Functional Resume—Skills and abilities listed under major skill categories. For instance, if you have excellent communication skills, "communication" is a category you could use.

Objective—Identifies the job position you are seeking. The objective is listed directly under the contact information.

References—Contact information of three people (preferably professionals) who can give you a positive recommendation. References are not located on the resume, but on a separate typed paper.

Reverse Chronological Resume or Chronological Resume—List your recent job first. The job before the recent job is listed second and so on. Job duties are included.

Silent "I"—The word I at the beginning of the sentence is understood but not used in resume writing. In Zen there is also no concept of I.

Skills Summary—Summary of your most important skills located at the top of the resume. The skills summary tells the employer what you can do for the employer not what the employer can do for you.

Appendix: C
Sample Job Application

Date_____

Company Name_____

Position Desired_____

Name_____
  First   Last

Address_____
       Number   Street   City/State/Zip

Social Security Number_____

Are you 18 years of age or older? _____

I am seeking (Circle one): Part-Time, Full-Time, Temporary, Seasonal work.

Best time of day to contact you_____

Have you ever worked for this company before? _____ If yes, when and where_____

Do you have any mental or physical condition which may limit your ability to do the job? _____ If yes, what can be changed to accommodate your limitation? _____

Have you ever been convicted of a crime? _____ If yes, **explain:** Felony, discuss at interview, including special skills and accomplishments.

Name Three References (Do not include relatives):

Name	Address	Phone Number

List any special skills:

_____

_____

_____

_____

Appendix: D
Action Verbs

assured	doubled	inspected	produced
attained	dramatized	installed	promoted
attended	drove	instilled	proved
balanced	educated	intensified	publicized
boosted	elected	intervened	purchased
briefed	eliminated	interview	questioned
budgeted	enacted	invested	raised
capitalized on	endorsed	judged	ranked
cared for	engineered	justified	realized
cataloged	enlarged	launched	received
centralized	ensured	lectured	recorded
checked	escalated	listened	redeemed
closed	estimated	located	redesigned
coined	examined	lowered	reduced
collected	exceeded	manipulated	reevaluated
comforted	exhibited	marketed	refined
commended	expedited	maximized	rehabilitated
communicated	experimented	mechanized	related
compared	explored	merged	remodeled
composed	expressed	ministered	renewed
conceived	extracted	moderated	replaced
concluded	facilitated	modified	reported

confined	filed	monitored	researched
consolidated	financed	motivated	resolved
contracted	focused	nominated	restored
controlled	forced	nurtured	retrieved
converted	forecasted	observed	reviewed
corrected	formulated	offered	revived
created	found	opened	safe guarded
customized	fulfilled	orchestrated	screened
decided	funded	originated	selected
decorated	grew	outlined	serviced
defined	guaranteed	overhauled	shaped
delivered	guided	oversaw	shipped
demonstrated	handled	participated	simplified
depicted	headed	perfected	solved
designed	helped	persuaded	spearheaded
detailed	hired	pinpointed	spelled out
devised	identified	placed	sponsored
dictated	imagined	positioned	standardized
disciplined	impressed	predicted	stated
supported			
surveyed			
synthesized			
tested			
targeted			
terminated			
traced			
trained			
transcribed			

transformed

treated

triumphed

tutored

unearthed

united

upheld

upgraded

vacated

verbalized

vitalized

won

wrote

Appendix: E
Helpful Resources

Social Security Card

To replace a lost card contact:

Social Security Administration
Office of Public Inquiries
Windsor Park Building
6401 Security Blvd.
Baltimore, MD 21235
1.800.772.1213
www.ssa.gov

National <u>H</u>elping <u>I</u>ndividuals with criminal records <u>Re</u>-enter through <u>E</u>mployment (H.I.R.E.) Network

H.I.R.E. Network is a national resource designed to help ex-offenders find quality employment and legal assistance. You will also find **Federal Bonding** and **Work Opportunity Tax Credit** information for all 50 states.
www.hirenetwork.org

Government Websites

Federal Bureau of Prisons
www.bop.gov

U.S. Department of Labor Employment & Training Administration
www.doleta.gov

U.S. Department of Justice Office of Justice Programs
www.ojp.usdoj.gov/reentry

U.S. Department of Veteran Affairs
www.va.gov

Legal Resources

Equal Employment Opportunity Commission (EEOC)
1801 L Street, NW
Washington, DC 20507
202.633.4900
1.800.669.4900
www.eeoc.gov
Government organization designed to enforce Title VII of the Civil Right Act of
1964. The Act prohibits employment discrimination.

Presidential Pardon

Pardon developed for individuals involved in a federal crime.
For more information write to:
Office of the Pardon Attorney U.S. Department of Justice
1425 New York Avenue, NW
Washington, DC 20530-0001
Applications can be obtained from the Pardon
Attorney's Web site:
www.usdoj.gov/pardon

Federal Student Financial Aid

To check eligibility for federal student financial aid call:
1.800.433.3243

or apply online at:

Free Application for Federal Student Aid (FAFSA)
www.fafsa.ed.gov

For more information concerning student
financial aid call for the Federal Student Aid Guide:

Federal Student Aid Information Center
1.800.433.3243
www.studentaid.ed.gov

Appendix: F
Further Reading
Resume and Job Search Books for
Formerly Incarcerated Persons

Resume Books

Enelow, Wendy S. Best Resumes & Letters for Ex-Offenders. Manassas Park, VA: Impact Publications, 2006.

Mendlin, Ronald C. Job Search Tools: Resumes, Applications, and Cover Letters. Indianapolis, IN: JIST, 2000.

Job Search/Job Hunting Tips

Jones, Louis. Man I Need a J-O-B! The Ex-Offender's Job Search Manual. Dallas, TX: OPEN, Inc., 2004.

Krannich, Ronald. Ex-Offender's Job Hunting Guide: 10 Steps to a New Life in the Work World. Manassas Park, VA: Impact Publications, 2005.

_____. Job Hunting Tips for People with Hot and Not-So-Hot Backgrounds. Manassas Park, VA: Impact Publications, 2005.

Lordan, Kathleen. Ex-Offender's Job Search Companion. Lawrenceville, NJ: Cambridge Educational, 2005.

Mendlin, Ronald C. Marc Polonsky. Being "Job Ready": Identify Your Skills, Strengths and Career Goals. Indianapolis, IN: JIST, 2000.

_____. "Double You": The Person You Are and the Person You Want to Be. Indianapolis, IN: JIST, 2000.

_____. Networking and Interviewing for Jobs. Indianapolis, IN: JIST, 2000.

Sull, Errol Craig. *Ex-Inmate's Complete Guide to Successful Employment.* Buffalo, NY: Aardvark Publishing, 2003.

Keeping a Job

Mendlin, Ronald C. *Keeping Your Job: Survive and Succeed in a New Job.* Indianapolis, IN: JIST, 2000.

Appendix: G
Further Reading
Interview Books

Adams, Bob. Everything Job Interview Book: Answer the Toughest Job Interview Questions with Confidence. Holbrook, MA: Adams Media, 2001.

Beatty, Richard H. Interview Kit. New York, NY: Wiley, 2000.

Block, Jay A. Great Answers! Great Questions! For Your Job Interview. New York, NY: McGraw-Hill, 2004.

Fry, Ronald W. 101 Great Answers to the Toughest Interview Questions. Franklin Lakes, NJ: Career Press, 2000.

Krannich, Caryl R. Job Interview Tips for People with Not-So-Hot Backgrounds: How to Put the Red Flags Behind You. Manassas Park, VA: Impact Publications, 2004.

Powers, Paul. Winning Job Interviews: Reduce Interview Anxiety Outprepare the Other Candidates, Land the Job You Love. Franklin Lakes, NJ: Career Press, 2005.

Appendix: H
Further Reading
General Job Search Books

Beck, Catherine B. It's Your Career Take Control! Palo Alto, CA: Davies-Black Publishing, 2004.

Bermont, Todd. 10 Insider Secrets to Job Hunting Success! Everything You Need to Know to Get the Job You Want. Chicago, IL: 10 Step Publications, 2002.

Bolles, Richard Nelson. What Color is Your Parachute? A Practical Manual for Job Hunters and Career Changers. Berkeley, CA: Ten Speed Press, 2007.

Farr, Michael. Getting the Job You Really Want: A Step-by-Step Guide to Finding a Good Job in Less Time. Indianapolis, IN: JIST Works, 2002.

Garber, Janet. I Need a Job, Now What?! New York, NY: Silver Lining Books, 2001.

Geary, Gail. Over-40 Job Search Guide: 10 Strategies for Making Your Age an Advantage in Your Career. Indianapolis, IN: JIST Works, 2005.

Hayden, C.J. Get Hired Now! A 28-Day Program for Landing the Job You Want. Berkeley, CA: Bay Tree Publishing, 2005.

Krannich, Ronald L. No One Will Hire Me: Avoid 15 Mistakes and Win the Job. Manassas Park, VA: Impact Publications, 2004.

Morem, Susan. How to Get a Job and Keep It: Career and Life Skills You Need to Succeed. Chicago, IL: Ferguson Publishing, 2002.

Appendix: I
Further Reading
General Resume Books

Beatty, Richard H. How to Write a Resume if You didn't go to College. Hoboken, NJ: Wiley Publishers, 2003.

Enelow, Wendy S. Best Resumes for People Without a Four Year Degree. Manassas Park, VA: Impact Publications, 2004.

_____. Expert Resumes for People Returning to Work. Indianapolis, IN: JIST Works, 2003.

Noble, David F. Gallery of Best Resumes for People Without a Four Year Degree. Indianapolis, IN: JIST Works, 2005.

Parker, Yana. Damn Good Resume Guide. Berkeley, CA: Ten Speed Press, 2002.

Public Library Association. Guide to Basic Resume Writing. Chicago, IL: VGM Career Books, 2004.

Resumes for College Students and Recent Graduates. New York, NY: VGM Career Books, 2005.

Resumes for the 50+ Job Hunter. Chicago, IL: VGM Career Books, 2003.

Resumes for Mid-Career Job Changers. Lincolnwood, Illinois: VGM Career Horizons, 2000.

Ryan, Robin. Winning Resumes. New York, NY: Wiley Publishers, 2003.

Appendix: J
Further Reading
Zen and Buddhism Books

✦

Here are some of my favorite books on Zen Buddhism, Buddhism in general, and books with Buddhist concepts. Enjoy!

Zen Buddhism Books

Hanh, Thich Nhat. The Long Road Turns to Joy: A Guide to Walking Meditation. Berkeley, CA: Parallax Press, 1996.

Levin, Daniel. The Zen Book. Carlsbad, CA: Hay House 2005.

McClain, Gary R. Complete Idiot's Guide to Zen Living. New York, NY: Alpha Books, 2001.

Sach, Jack. Everything Zen Book: Achieve Inner Calm and Peace of Mind through Meditation, Simple Living, and Harmony. Avon, MA: Adams Media Corporation, 2004.

Sell, Colleen. 10 Minute Zen: Easy Tips to Lead You Down the Path of Enlightenment. Gloucester, MA: Fair Winds Press, 2002.

Smith, Jean. The Beginner's Guide to Zen Buddhism. New York, NY: Bell Tower, 2000.

Buddhism Books

Gach, Gary. Complete Idiot's Guide to Understanding Buddhism. Indianapolis, IN: Alpha Books, 2002.

Lowenstein, Tom. Buddhist Inspirations. Winchester, Hampshire, United Kingdom: Duncan Baird Publishers, 2005.

Timuss, Christopher. Light on Enlightenment: Revolutionary Teachings on the Inner Life. Boston, MA: Shambhala Publications, 1998.

Buddhism and Healing

Rinpoche, Dagsay Tulku. The Practice of Tibetan Meditation. Exercises, Visualizations, and Mantras for Health and Well-Being. Rochester, VT: Inner Traditions International, 2002.

Thondup, Tulku. Healing Power of Mind: Simple Meditation Exercises for Health, Well Being, and Enlightenment. Boston, MA: Shambhala, 1996.

Buddhist Concepts

Chopra, Deepak. Journey into Healing: Awakening the Wisdom Within You. New York, NY: Harmony Books, 1994.

_____. Seven Spiritual Laws of Success: A Practical Guide to the Fulfillment of Your Dreams. San Rafael, CA: Amber-Allen Publishing, 1994.

Kehoe, John. Mind Power into the 21st Century: Techniques to Harness the Astounding Powers of Thought. West Vancouver, British Columbia, Canada: Zoetic, 1997.

Appendix: K
Further Reading
Keyword Books

Block, Jay A., Michael Betrus. 2500 Keywords to Get You Hired. New York, NY: McGraw-Hill, 2003.

Enelow, Wendy S. Best Keywords for Resumes, Cover Letters, and Interviews: Powerful Communication Tools for Success. Manassas Park, VA: Impact Publications, 2003.

_____. Keywords to Nail Your Job Interview. Manassas Park, VA: Impact Publications, 2004.

Herman, Erik, Sarah Rocha. Resume Buzz Words. Avon, MA: Adams Media, 2005.

Appendix: L
Further Reading
Books that Describe Occupations
and Provide Earning
Information

Encyclopedia of Careers and Vocational Guidance. New York, NY: Facts on File, 2005.

Farr, Michael, Laurence Shatkin. O*Net Dictionary of Occupational Titles. Indianapolis, IN: JIST Works, 2005.

____. 250 Best Jobs through Apprenticeships. Indianapolis, IN: JIST Works, 2005

Krannich, Ron, Caryl Krannich. America's Top 100 Jobs for People Without a Four Year Degree. Manassas Park, VA: Impact Publications, 2005.

Occupational Outlook Handbook. Washington, DC: U.S. Department of Labor, Bureau of Labor Statistics, 2006.

Rich, Jason R. 202 High-Paying Jobs You Can Land Without a College Degree. Irvine, CA: Entrepreneur Press, 2006.

Bibliography
Works Cited

Bureau of Justice Statistics. "Prison Statistics." June 2005. U.S. Department of Justice. 21 July 2006 <http://www.ojp.usdoj.gov/bjs/prisons.htm>.

Byrom, Thomas. Dhammapada: The Saying of the Buddha. Boston, MA: Shambhala Publications, 1993.

Enelow, Wendy S., Ronald Krannich. Best Resumes & Letters for Ex-Offenders. Manassas Park VA: Impact Publications, 2006.

Levin, Daniel. The Zen Book. Carlsbad, CA: Hay House, Inc: 2005.

National Center for Complementary and Alternative Medicine. "BackGrounder: Meditation for Health Purposes." February 2006. National Institutes of Health. 21 July 2006. <http://nccam.nih.gov/health/meditation>.

About the Author

Through lovingkindness Simone Richardson developed the compassion to help others. Simone's compassion was enhanced with her creation of resume workshops for the general public, her creation of an ex-offender job search resource for the public, her interest in and practice of Zen, and the encouragement of two coworkers. One coworker told Simone that she should write a book. Another coworker told Simone that helping ex-offenders was Simone's ministry, and that her ministry should stretch far beyond the walls of her job. Simone's response to the two recommendations resulted in the development of this resource.

Simone earned a B.A. in Communicative Disorders, and a M.A. in Communication from The University of Akron, Akron, Ohio. She holds a Master of Library Science degree from Kent State University, Kent, Ohio. An avid "person, who meditates," Simone currently works as a librarian in Akron, Ohio.

Om mani padme hum
Buddhist mantra

978-0-595-42312-5
0-595-42312-4